before this massive prison block. Our heads and our hearts raced with new and confusing emotions. What could *we* do—the three of us against the dark forces of Communism?

THREE BEHIND
THE CURTAIN

*by Sammy Tippit
as told to
Jerry B. Jenkins*

Whitaker House
ONE U.A.M. SQUARE
PITTSBURGH and COLFAX STS., SPRINGDALE, PA 15144

ISBN: 0-88368-068-8

WHITAKER HOUSE
1 U.A.M. Square
Springdale, Pennsylvania 15144

© 1975 by Whitaker House

Printed in the United States of America

To Fred Bishop and Fred Starkweather,
and my brothers and sisters
behind the iron curtain.
                                    S.T.

And for Jim, Jeff, and Jay.
                                    J.J.

CONTENTS

FOREWORD

There is great confusion among the people of America about the existing religious situation in the communist countries. Some speak of religious freedom, while others say that communist countries are closed for evangelization.

After a meeting in San Antonio, Texas, a few years ago, a young man came to me and told me that he was getting ready to go behind the iron curtain to preach the Gospel. His name was Sammy Tippit. Because I had spent thirteen years in communist prisons, this was especially interesting to me.

In reading his book, THREE BEHIND THE CURTAIN, about his experiences while behind the iron curtain, I was thrilled to see how God used this young preacher of the Gospel to deliver the message of salvation to the most forgotten and abandoned missionary field in the world. Such books are a great help in revealing the truth about the real religious situation behind the iron curtain.

My prayer is that this book will be used to bring great blessing to many who read it, to challenge God's people in America to pray for the Christians in Communist-dominated lands who struggle for survival and suffer constant persecution, and to inspire other consecrated Christians to follow Sammy's example.

Haralan Popov
Author of *Tortured for His Faith*

Part One

THE CALL

Chapter One

A WHOPPER OF A VISION

No one else saw what I saw in that *Burger King* restaurant. Not even Tex, my wife of a few months.

As I sat there in Baton Rouge, munching on my *Whopper* and gazing out the big glass windows, my mind carried me far beyond the borders of Louisiana.

Strangely shivering on such a warm evening, I stared straight ahead. Chairs scraped the floor, mothers scolded rowdy children, and Tex brushed her lips with a napkin. But I was somewhere else. The restaurant had been transported across the ocean. My *Coke* had become a hot drink, maybe coffee or cocoa. The people around me were speaking a language I couldn't understand. Realizing that I was behind the iron curtain (in my mind), surrounded by people who were locked in a godless vacuum, I bled for them and burned to tell

13

them the "forbidden news." The vision was so real, I knew it must have some special meaning; it stayed with me for several days.

It was 1968. I had been reading about the persecution of Christian believers behind the iron curtain, and God had laid them on my heart, constantly reminding me to pray for them. I even sent a little money to some organizations sponsoring ministries there. But now I felt God calling *me* to go. But how could I? I was just twenty-one. Our home in Walker, Louisiana, was a long way from Europe. Yet I thought of the vision daily. I knew God wanted me to go.

Only recently God had called me to quit college in my senior year and to minister on the streets. He had brought me far in the Word and had taught me much of Himself. But now I was frustrated. When would He lead me to Europe? How would He provide? I could only share my burden with friends and wait.

Some young people at the Walker Baptist Church caught my enthusiasm and wanted to help. The seventy-two dollars they raised with a car wash didn't get me far, but I put the money away and cherished it as their expression of love. One day I would use it.

When I checked with travel agencies and found that getting to Europe would cost seven or eight hundred dollars, I began to doubt that God had been the author of my vision. *Maybe this isn't the time,* I told myself. Months later I would realize that God had much to teach me before entrusting me with an iron curtain ministry.

Though I was a bit puzzled by the vision and the lack of anything materializing from it, it seemed to pop into my mind often enough to keep a fire kindled within me for the persecuted be-

14

lievers and the spiritually lost people behind the curtain.

Then came our crash course in "Iron Curtain Basics." First Tex and I had to learn to live totally by faith. To get us started, God sent us and five friends on a walk from Monroe, Louisiana, to Washington, D.C., where we met and held a prayer and fast vigil with Arthur Blessitt. God had blessed my preaching ministry since the day I had yielded to Him my speaking ability as a new Christian, and I was given many opportunities to preach during the "faith walk." (In high school I had been named the outstanding youth speaker in North America by the United Nations, never having any idea that I would one day be speaking for God.)

Next Tex and I were led to set up our *God's Love in Action* ministry in Chicago, and for two years God taught us patience. Not only patience to wait for His timing concerning the iron curtain, but patience in seeing results on the streets of Chicago. That was a tough lesson. We had seen immediate results of witnessing in the South, but God brought us through some lean times in Chicago before pouring out His Spirit and moving mightily through us. Finally the fireworks started though, and our exciting and dramatic ministry in Chicago eventually led to our taking on two other couples and six young people for a full-time staff.

Then we had to learn some financial lessons. I was convinced, and still am, that God will provide for His own, through His own. God's people will take care of His servants. But I am often tempted to worry when the funds seem to be running short. During the rough Chicago days when there were a dozen mouths to feed, our son

15

was born and countless other expenses piled up. But God moved His people to care for us.

I had promised God that we would never ask for money. I had been called to preach Christ, not to raise funds. I believed that as long as I obeyed Him, I could be confident that my God would supply all my needs according to His riches in Christ Jesus.

The lessons learned in Chicago would be invaluable to us when we finally made our first trip to Europe, but I was still impatient about it. *When, Lord? When will you send me to the calling I know you have for me?*

Once during our two years in Chicago I was to speak at the World Home Bible League. Pastors from Poland and Romania spoke before I did, but I heard hardly a word. Their accents, their demeanor sent my head and my heart across the ocean. This time I was experiencing more of a daydream than a vision, but my heart cried out for the world. My scope had broadened and my burden became one for a dying world. The needs of Chicago were overwhelming enough —but here I was feeling for the entire world! People were dying and going to hell. I had the Answer and I wanted to share it.

Daily the burden grew, but still nothing materialized. So we continued on with the Chicago ministry, not realizing that the persecution we faced was also part of the necessary preparation. I was hassled constantly and was at one point even arrested and jailed for sharing my faith on the street. We came through nearly two years of gut level ministering, reaching the kids on the street during the week and preaching at different churches almost every weekend.

We were at the height of our Chicago outreach late in 1971 when I knelt one night to pray with Murray Bradfield, a close associate. Kids by the dozens had come to Christ and had left the streets to join our weekly Bible study sessions. We had been through every imaginable trial from threats to power shortages, and now God chose to speak. As Murray and I prayed, I glanced at the world map we had hung on the wall. It was as if a light had been focused on the slogan penned above it: *The World For Jesus*. God spoke clearly to my heart. It was time to go.

Money seemed to come in from everywhere, and the last $2500 was given to us by a school-teacher who said God had told Him to offer his life savings. It was just the amount we needed, and we left for Germany, praising God.

Berlin was a whole new world. During a week's vigil of fasting and prayer at the Kaiser Wilhelm War Memorial Church in West Berlin, I visited a pastor from a nearby church. On my way back to the Wilhelm Church I ducked into a coffee shop to evade the icy winter winds. As I sat sipping hot chocolate I suddenly recognized the setting. The glassed-in restaurant. Sipping a hot drink. Shivering a bit. People all around me speaking a foreign tongue. This was it! The confirmation of my vision.

God had led me there to assure me that His hand would be upon my ministry and that this, the only free city in a Communistic country, would be an important and strategic one in my future. With the realization of the vision came that gripping burden for the people. As I glanced about me I saw the faces and the weary bodies of lost souls. My whole being ached for their salvation and I was moved to tears.

I left quickly and hurried back to the Wilhelm Church to share God's blessing with Murray and the others. God gave me a love for the city of Berlin, and I became convinced that it affords one of the rare ministering opportunities of our time. With the security check being light, and the freedom of Americans to go into the Communist side on twenty-four-hour visas, Berlin becomes an easy city in which to share Christ.

Becoming familiar with this city was important for me for more reasons than I could understand then. God was preparing me for the Communist Youth World Fest, but I wasn't even aware of it yet.

I was led to carry a cross from Munich to Kassal and then to Berlin, and it was on this walk that we first encountered hard core Communists.

I had memorized the *Four Spiritual Laws* in German, as well as a few verses of Scripture. While I felt terribly inadequate with the language, God blessed my enthusiasm and two Africans received Christ through my witness at the University of Munich on the first day of our walk.

As I stood talking with the Africans I noticed a large group of students gathering around. They had tables full of signs and literature hawking their particular political stands. It blew my mind. In America, where people *think* there is healthy political interest and debate, you'd never see anything like this. There were Chinese-oriented Communists, Russian-oriented Communists, and Marxists, all arguing among themselves. Their zeal and intensity impressed me, and we blitzed their debate, passing out tracts and talking with as many as we could about the claims of Christ. There we were, in Free Germany, getting a taste of Communism. What must occupied Germany be like?

We began to draw larger and larger crowds wherever we were given a chance to speak. *Living Water*, our singing group, would sing and play, then Murray would share his testimony and I would preach. We learned that if there is one thing the Communists fear, it's an outpouring of the Holy Spirit. Wherever we spoke, people flocked in to see what it was all about. And when the Communists realized what we were doing, they came in and tried to stifle our witness.

In Neu-Isenburg, near Frankfurt, we were confronted by a group of students from the University of Frankfurt who had obviously been very well organized by professors. We were speaking to one of our largest crowds and *Living Water* was singing when a group of Communists started chanting, "We want discussion! We want discussion!"

We had a huge sound system, but the Communists were so numerous and loud that they even drowned out the music. When Murray stepped up to give his testimony, the chanting grew louder and he could not be heard. He looked directly at the Communists and spoke quietly. They hesitated for an instant to see if he would try to shout them down or order them to leave. "Jesus liebt dich," he said. (Jesus loves you.)

They were astonished and fell silent. But when he finished speaking and the music began again, so did the chanting. "Power to the people! We want discussion! Power to the People!" I didn't know what kind of response my preaching would get.

When the interpreter and I stepped to the microphone, the noise was deafening. A member of *Living Water* and two Christian soldiers moved quickly into the midst of the Communists and knelt to pray. The Communists were freaked out. They ran to their leader and asked what to do, but by then I had the attention of the rest of the crowd.

About a dozen received Christ that night, and when I returned to the auditorium from the counseling room the crowd had remained and was in an uproar. The news media were there, and everyone seemed to be demanding debate. I don't generally allow debate of the Gospel; in America this would usually wind up in an endless nit-picking discussion.

But this was a different atmosphere. All kinds of people were there. The Spirit seemed to be leading, and this crowd was likely to come up with very direct and clear challenges, answerable if God would give me divine wisdom. Silently I prayed for that as I said, "All right. We'll have debate, but we'll have order. If there is any disorder, we'll quit."

As the questions began I felt clearly the presence of God. I had never studied dialectical materialism or even Communism much for that matter, but the Lord was making me sensitive to the arguments, and I was able to see past the words and into the real problems.

I was wearing a vest with *Jesus Loves You* sewn on the back. One of the first questions was more of a charge. "I'll bet you supported a big, capitalist company by purchasing that vest!"

"No," I answered. "My wife made this because we wanted to share what we had with others."

20

Much of the crowd, even some Communists, applauded. Praise God.

"Are there white churches in America which won't allow blacks in?"

"There may be, but not my church," I said. "A few years ago I had hatred in my heart for blacks, but when I met Jesus He replaced that hatred with love. If you want to bring the races together, the love of God will do it."

For several minutes the questions were hurled, but God gave me wisdom to answer each. The crowd's applause with each answer befuddled the Communists. An American pastor in the crowd told the European Baptist Press that it was the greatest outpouring of the Spirit he had ever seen in his years in the ministry.

When we finally reached the end of our walk across Germany I spoke at a series of pre-planned rallies in West Berlin, and we received national television coverage. God had moved and had wonderfully blessed our ministry there, but being so close to the border made me hungry to get past the wall into East Berlin. It was why I had come.

A young man I had met in Chicago was studying in Berlin and was working with *Youth With A Mission* in Europe (I cannot divulge his name. I'll call him Jeff.) He agreed to take Murray, Debbie Bradfield, Tex, our two-month-old Davey, and me to visit some believers behind the iron curtain.

I had been burdened for the persecuted Christians for years. My vision had been confirmed three years from that day in the Baton Rouge *Burger King,* and now I was to go behind the curtain. I could hardly wait.

Chapter Two

THE WALL

I'll never forget the first time I saw the wall. I wouldn't want to if I could.

We climbed upon a little stand at Checkpoint Charlie from which I could see the mine fields planted on the other side. Every seventy-five yards or so was a huge tower on the East side where a machine gunner watched. His assignment: kill his own countrymen who tried to escape.

I was helpless before this massive prison block. My head and my heart raced with new and confusing emotions. I had never seen anything like it in my life, and I haven't since. It was incredible, and it tore me up inside. What could *I* do, a little nobody against the forces of Communism —indeed, the forces of Satan?

I paced, staring at the gut-wrenching scene, my heart crying within me, "O God, how can we reach these people for Jesus Christ? There must be some way we can reach out to them with the

Good News." I couldn't remember ever having been so moved.

We chose to cross the border with Jeff, not at Checkpoint Charlie, but via train through Friedrech Strasse. The guards looked us over closely and we filled out cards telling where we were from, why we were visiting East Berlin, where we would be staying, and how much money we were bringing. The whole thing made me nervous, but I would get used to it in the ensuing years.

Once we were through and had arrived in East Berlin I was relieved. But another mind blowing experience was seeing the contrast between the East and West sides. West Berlin is full of life and light and gaiety, but the East side is tomblike.

There was no noise in the dank, dimly lit streets. Everything was gray. My relief at being finished with the border check was replaced by the creeps. I was afraid, anxious, burdened, loving, all at the same time. I could hardly sort out my emotions as the impact of the city washed over me.

Jeff took us to visit a wonderful old Christian man whom I'll call Pastor Schmidt. The old man had been imprisoned during the Hitler regime for refusing to instruct his Lutheran congregation to bow to the Führer. I found Pastor Schmidt a warm and wonderful man. He was so excited about talking with fellow believers that his Russian and his German would sometimes get mixed together with his English as he excitedly told stories of how God had blessed his boldness. We just sat enthralled with his experiences.

He had circulated an underground letter to his Lutheran pastor colleagues, begging them not to sign a state document calling Communism the savior of the world. The Communists did not mind him preaching that Jesus was *a* personal savior, but Pastor Schmidt and the others were forbidden to preach Christ as *the* Savior of the world. All were to sign, and all but Pastor Schmidt did sign.

What a tremendous blessing this man of God was to us! And he was still active. He was studying Russian so he could share Christ with the Russian soldiers, even at the risk of imprisonment again. Holy boldness.

Pastor Schmidt took us to a Lutheran church that Sunday morning, and again I was forced to add yet another emotion to my frazzled brain. I saw hardly any young people. Here was a nation of lost souls who needed to be reached for Jesus, and the church was full of old, tired, beaten people. I felt for them, and I could feel little but pity for them, but certainly there were few among them who were equipped to win their countrymen for God.

I was encouraged that evening when we went to an *Evangelische Frei Kirche* (Evangelical Free Church). All "Evangelical Free" means in Germany is that it is not hooked up with either the Catholic or Lutheran groups, the two state churches. This church was filled with young people, and thus with life and joy. We were really blessed and encouraged by that service, just to know that there was a core of young people who would defy the state and exercise their faith in a free church. It was a risk for them, but their intensity was obvious.

As we rode the train back from the services, Pastor Schmidt pointed out a group of young people traveling together. They were all wearing blue uniforms. "There are some Free German Youth," Pastor Schmidt said.

"What's that?" we asked. "What is the Free German Youth?"

The old man shook his head slowly and with a wry smile he said, "They're not really free. They either go along with that Communistic organization, the FGY, or they cannot continue their education. That's really free, isn't it?"

As the train rattled up to the border, we could see Checkpoint Charlie. Pastor Schmidt just gazed at the wall and his thoughts seemed far away. We left the train and he took us to a spot called the Temple of Tears, the spot where you cross the border on the way back. It got its name because of the tears shed there by the countless parting relatives.

It was hard to leave the old man. He hugged and kissed us and our eyes filled with tears. He looked up at the towers and said to me, "Someday maybe I will be able to visit you on the other side."

He tried to smile. "I sure hope so," I said. "I really do hope you'll be able to."

We left Pastor Schmidt not knowing what would happen to him. Would we ever see him again? Would it be in the East or in the West? If in the East, would it be at his home, or in a prison? Here was a bold man who loved the Lord. Our hearts bled for him.

For days I couldn't shake the rapid-fire experiences and emotions I had been through during our visit to East Berlin. The things we had seen, the people we had met, the churches we had been in, Pastor Schmidt, the grayness of the streets, the constant feeling of oppression. And the words of Pastor Schmidt echoed in my mind, "Someday, maybe I will be able to visit you on the other side."

On Christmas Eve, 1971, Tex and I were thousands of miles from home and family. "Let's go to the wall," I told her. We said nothing as we walked that night. I just cried. The impact of the wall had lost none of its intensity. I was shaken anew with the overwhelming burden of these people—the believers and the lost. "God," I prayed, "allow me to reach those people for Jesus Christ. Though they be in a great prison cell, I pray that one day they might be set free by the power of the resurrected Christ."

I didn't know what God had in store for us. I knew only that we returned to Chicago with a burden that would not be forgotten. Something was in my heart for East Germany which would not leave. I longed to know what God had for us to do there.

Chapter Three

PREPARATION

We moved our headquarters from Chicago to Miami, Florida, mainly because we felt led to carry out a concentrated witness at the 1972 national political conventions there. But something in the back of my mind told me that it would be only temporary; though I felt a tremendous burden for the United States and its political leaders, deep inside I was being drawn back to Germany. For some reason, God had called me there, and it was hard to think of anything else.

We enjoyed the blessing of God at the conventions. Meanwhile, Murray and Debbie Bradfield were heading up a unique ministry at the Munich olympics. They had stayed in Germany to follow up converts (along with another member of our staff, a young man named Chris). I was anxious to get back overseas to see how everything had gone and to get to the job to which

God had called us. In September of 1972, most of the staff we had in Miami left to begin similar ministries of their own, and it seemed that God was clearly calling us to move to Germany, at least for awhile.

Ricky Auxier and Don Price went with us to Germany, and the Bradfields and Chris would make up the rest of our complete staff. I was so excited about talking to Murray in Luxembourg after having not seen him for nine months that we stayed up almost all night to share what God had been doing in our lives. We were like little kids, laughing and praising God for the unusual and thrilling experiences He had brought us through.

Tex, Davey, and I made our home in Walldorf, a little town near the Frankfurt International Airport and just 10 minutes from downtown Frankfurt by train. Don, Ricky, Murray, and I sent several days in prayer, seeking the will of God, and God opened the door for me to minister in one of the schools in nearby Russelsheim. (I will not always be able to divulge the specific avenues through which we were allowed to witness.)

Every day I would speak to five or six classes at the school, and at night I would preach in a church and many of the kids from the school would come to the meetings. Many were saved, and God was really blessing that witness.

As we were to find constantly in Germany, the kids were extremely politically minded. Speaking on that level was just about the only way to reach them. Time after time I spoke on revolutionizing the world, through the supreme Revolutionist.

Though God was blessing, I constantly felt inadequate in the new surroundings. The feeling of alienation nearly overwhelmed me, so it seemed that any time I wasn't preaching, I was praying.

One day while Murray, Ricky, Don, and I were praying, the Holy Spirit very clearly impressed upon me to memorize my testimony in German. I asked Murray to help me, because by this time he had really picked up a lot of German.

I wrote my testimony in English and then Murray translated into German, explaining the pronunciation of every syllable for me, until I could recite it clearly. He also explained the sentence structure so I could use the correct inflection. With the few verses of Scripture I had memorized, and the *Four Spiritual Laws,* my testimony became the extent of my German vocabulary. I wasn't sure why I had been led to memorize it. In fact, I often wondered about that. I had always had access to good interpreters.

Berlin beckoned me. I had fallen in love with that city, and I was anxious to return. It had been nearly a year since Tex and I had prayed and cried at the wall. We had purchased two Volkswagens soon after we arrived (shocking the townfolk by paying cash. They thought we were just a bunch of irresponsible kids—"Jesus People.")

We took off for Berlin in the autos God had provided through the gifts of His people. We were really checked thoroughly at the border since we were traveling by car, and it was a whole new experience for Don and Ricky. As we were finally cleared for passage, the last border guard was a girl who said, "You can go now." I looked at her and was glad to be able to say those three words I had heard Murray use so often: "Jesus liebt dich."

In West Berlin we held a meeting at a church where the pastor became a close brother. I'll call him Pastor Haase. The entire Haase family was wonderful to us and we had great fellowship with them. Often the simple German choruses and songs we sang with them will come back to me and I'll sing them to myself in German. We always had blessed times of sharing, singing, and eating with the Haases.

I was anxious to get to the wall again. It was another first for Ricky and Don, and their experience was the same as mine had been. It broke their hearts.

God spoke to me anew. "Sammy," He spoke to my heart, "you've got to reach out to the young people behind the iron curtain." I could sense the massiveness of their number.

I knew there were Christian groups supplying Bibles and literature for the believers, but I knew of no one who was actively reaching the population of lost young people. "God," I prayed, "please let me do that."

What a thrill it was to go behind the curtain again and to visit Pastor Schmidt. When he opened the door he broke into tears and threw his arms around us. There was so much to share after having not seen each other for almost a year. He said that he had become more fluent with Russian and was being given many opportunities to witness to Russian military personnel on trains and on the street.

After we had fellowshipped in his home, he took us to a Russian military base where we saw a movie depicting the Russian occupation of East Berlin. Of course, it was from their viewpoint. It was a strange experience for us as Americans to be sitting in an enemy military base watching one of their own propaganda films.

As we left the base, something told me that I would return one day to share Christ there. I didn't know when, why, or how. I just knew.

Pastor Schmidt took us again to the Evangelical Free Church, the one in which we had enjoyed the service the year before. This night they were having a testimony service. Jeff, our friend from *Youth With a Mission*, went forward and shared his testimony.

As he spoke my heart pounded. God seemed to be saying, "Go ahead and give your testimony. This is your opportunity. This is why you have memorized your testimony."

I was scared. There were no interpreters here. In West Berlin, English is the second language to German, but here in the German Democratic Republic (East Berlin), Russian is the second language.

I felt locked to my seat. I wanted to share my testimony, yet I was torn. Had I memorized it well enough? Would the people respond? Suddenly the pastor looked at me and pointed. "Du, du," he said. *You, you,* he was saying. God had led him to call on me to give my testimony. I went trembling.

This pastor, not even knowing who I was, had singled me out, so I knew it must be of God. I spoke out in German and the love of God filled me. As I talked I wasn't aware of how strange my accent might seem to the people, or of what they might be thinking of me. I was just loving them in Jesus and trying to share with them.

Many people came up later and hugged me and said in German, "We love you," "Praise

God," and other phrases of encouragement, some I couldn't understand. But I knew we were one in Christ. It seemed that I had been as much a blessing to them as it had been to me to be able to share with them. For me it was just further confirmation that God had great plans for us in Germany.

Chapter Four

MISSION: IMPOSSIBLE

Since the day of my vision in Baton Rouge, and through both trips to Germany I had longed to know the specific will of God concerning what we had been called to do behind the iron curtain. The Lord had blessed our witnessing and my preaching. Souls had come to Jesus, but I was always impressed with the knowledge that a tremendous, major assignment awaited us. I wondered if God felt that there was still more I needed to learn before He would reveal it to me.

That night after the service at the Evangelical Free Church where I had given my testimony, we returned to Pastor Schmidt's home for the usual coffee and cake they had for us. It had been an exhausting day, and I was really wiped out. Having had one too many of the filling pieces of cake, I nearly dozed off while Pastor Schmidt fellowshipped with the others.

Suddenly something he said shocked me back

into reality. "I want you to pray about coming back here next summer to preach at the Communist Youth World Fest."

"What?" I said, bolting upright. "What's that?"

My heart pounded as Pastor Schmidt explained. "There will be 100,000 young people in the city of Berlin from every Communist country in the world. These will be the elite Communist young people, many even from America and other free countries."

Pastor Schmidt said that he did not think the Communists would risk arresting any Christians since it would cause an international scene. And besides, the Communists would likely be billing the event as a gala freedom-of-expression affair. They probably wouldn't be terribly intolerant during its few days.

My heart burned within me as I realized that *this* was what God was calling me to. Here would be probably the greatest opportunity in history to minister behind the iron curtain, and possibly even without getting arrested.

"How can we get the details on this?" I asked Pastor Schmidt.

"Go through Alexanderplatz tomorrow to a travel agency. They will be able to tell you more. But be careful."

That night in bed on the free side of the border I just praised God. "Oh, thank you, Jesus for what you're going to do at the Communist Youth World Fest."

The next day Don, Ricky, and I went across the border. I was so excited to learn more about the World Fest that I could hardly concentrate; but I also knew that God had called us to minister to the Germans that day as well. We could get more details later; right now we should be witnessing to the young people on the trains. They made a captive audience. So many young people rode the trains that we spent most of the day just riding back and forth passing out tracts and witnessing. At the three- and four-minute stops I would just stand up and preach my testimony, then hop off and catch a train going the other way.

Often we would split up and share with people individually on the different cars and on different trains. We probably spoke personally with nearly a hundred that day. Almost every person I talked to told me that he had been taught that there was no God. It broke my heart, yet I could see the hunger in each young person's eyes. They wanted to hear more, yet they warned us of the police. One girl told Don, "You must not do this. If the police find out, you will be in very much trouble."

Not one young person was rude to us or turned us off. They had grown up in a situation where it was normal for everyone to share his particular political beliefs. They were used to listening, but this day they were hearing something they didn't expect to hear. They seemed more concerned with our safety than with theirs and often they left us saying, "I want to know more. I'm interested in hearing more." It was tremendous.

I was glad that we had spent much of the day witnessing, even though we needed to get more info on the World Fest. It was good for me to get one more confirmation that these people were hungry to hear the Word of God. My heart was encouraged and God seemed to be commanding me to reach the masses so that they could at least hear the other side.

I felt like Isaiah when he saw how unclean and unworthy he was for the task to which God was calling him. God had asked, "Who will go?" and Isaiah had answered, "Here am I Lord, send me." I saw the Lord lifted up on that train, and inwardly I again expressed my desire that He take me and use me to reach these people.

It was time to find out about the World Fest. Our next few hours could have been the makings for a low grade spy movie. We went through Alexanderplatz on the east side of the border and went to the agency Pastor Schmidt had told us about. We were sent to another office where the officials sent us to yet another building. Finally a girl began asking us questions.

"We're just interested in the World Fest because we might like to attend," I told her in German.

"Come with me," she said.

We followed her to the parking lot and she told us to wait in a car. We had not met anyone in East Berlin who owned an automobile, so we thought the whole scene was getting a bit unusual. When we had sat there for forty-five minutes with no further word, we really started to get spooked.

Finally a man came out and got behind the wheel without a word. He started the engine and drove off. We looked at each other, all thinking, *Oh, no. Is this a trap? Do they know what we're up to already?* Suddenly the driver spoke.

"That's the Russian embassy," he said, pointing. I didn't know what to say. He pulled in front of the building next to the one he had pointed out. After we all got out of the car,

36

he opened the door of the building for us and we filed in.

"You must sign in and you must give over your passports," we were told. I wasn't too anxious to let my passport go, but we were so far along in this crazy deal already that I figured we had better do whatever they said.

We walked down a long corridor and I noticed that there was an alarm device hooked to every door to prevent any unauthorized personnel from entering. Covering almost the entire wall of one of the rooms was a huge blow-up of Angela Davis. I didn't know what in the world we were into, but I knew it was one of the longest walks I'd ever taken.

We were led to a beautiful reception room full of French university students who all spoke very fluent English. They were there to communicate to English-speaking people interested in the Fest. They sat us down and served us tea, making every attempt to make us feel comfortable. They failed. We felt miserable. And scared.

A man who seemed to be a host came up after a few moments and asked, "Well now, what can we tell you about the Communist Youth World Fest?"

"Well," I said, "we just want to know when it will be and how we can be involved, because we thought we might like to come."

He didn't seem the least bit suspicious of us, but we were sure wary of him and them and the whole place. They gave us sheets full of information on the Fest and thanked us for our interest. We were never asked the exact nature of our interest, and of course we never offered.

As we walked back to the waiting car, each vowed to the other that he would not get involved in anything like this again. I was glad to get my passport back. As we stepped into the sunlight I noticed that the girl who had led us to the car initially was waiting for us. She rode back with us to the original building. Before we parted I felt the Spirit leading me to give her a *Four Spiritual Laws* booklet.

I hesitated. "Oh, Lord, I can't do that," I prayed silently. "She's part of the Communist party."

The Spirit rebuked me, impressing upon my heart that if we came to the Communist Youth World Fest, everyone we encountered would be a member of the Communist party. I handed her the booklet. "Jesus liebt dich," I said.

She did a doubletake, staring at me. Then she smiled. "Danke," she said. (Thank you.) And she walked away.

The three of us ran for the train, not knowing whether to laugh or pray. "From now on let's leave the finding out of information to someone else!" we all agreed.

I knew that God had brought us from Frankfurt to Berlin just to learn of the Fest and to begin preparing for that mission. Tex and I headed back for Frankfurt, taking Ricky and Don with us so we could drop them off at Frankfurt International Airport in time to catch their flight to the States. We all had a lot to think and talk and pray about. We didn't know what the future held for Don and Ricky, or whether they were to join me in the Fest ministry or not. But God had worked in all of our lives. And I, for one, had finally realized a definite calling for the next summer.

I had one more important lesson to learn, and I would learn it that very week.

Chapter Five

THE COVERING

We decided to drive through East Germany to Frankfurt at night because Davey could sleep, and we could trade off driving. It turned out to be a mistake. I got confused and got on the wrong highway ,which in East Germany is illegal. They are very careful about who they let on which highway, and here I was lost. I took an exit and then another road hoping to get onto the right road, but suddenly I found myself in the middle of a Russian military base.

"Lord," I prayed aloud, "get us out of here and I'll never be stupid enough to try to drive across East Germany at night again." We finally got turned around and onto the right highway, but for a while I thought our iron curtain ministry had been ended before it got started. We were sure glad to get back to Frankfurt.

After Ricky and Don left, Murray and Debbie

decided that they would like to visit the States for a few weeks too. Suddenly Tex, Davey, and I were alone. There was no staff. No friends. No nothing.

One day the mail brought a notice from the police. From what I could understand, it was very important that they talk with me that day. *Oh, no,* I thought. *We were seen in the Russian military base, and now we're in big trouble.*

My German still wasn't the best and I didn't understand much of what was said at the police station. Tex and Davey were with me, and I kept looking to Tex to see if she could figure what they were trying to say. She couldn't. They had people scurrying in and out and checking on things. Finally they tried to make it easy for me.

They made some drawings of two cars on the highway and pointed to one following another. "Is this your car?" they asked.

Oh, now they've got us. I wasn't about to lie. "Yes," I said.

"Then it's very important that you come back tonight with an interpreter and sign a confession."

Now our ministry is ruined, I just know it.

That evening I took with me a man we had met named Helmut who spoke both English and German. He helped me write out a complete confession that it was indeed my car that had gotten off the main highway and had entered the Russian military base. As I finished and handed it to the police, fearing the worst, Helmut spoke up.

"Sammy, what time did you say this happened?"

"Late at night, about midnight I guess."

40

"Then something is wrong. They are talking about something which happened in the middle of the day."

I was totally confused. Helmut began talking to the police in German. As it turned out, all the police wanted me for was to tell them about a wreck I was supposed to have witnessed on the highway. I was so sure that they had seen us in the military base that I had 'fessed up to something they weren't concerned about at all. We all had a good laugh over it, but I was weak-kneed by the time we got back home and realized how foolish I had been.

The fear of losing my ministry was so real that it scared me into rethinking our whole setup. I began to realize that our ministry was not "covered" spiritually by a local body of believers. Sure the incident on the highway had been a humorous one, but it was also of God because I think He wanted to teach me something important without making me suffer for it.

I had experienced the fullness of the Holy Spirit more than four years before, and I knew how to witness, I had the power to witness and to preach, but I didn't have the authority which would have come from being covered by a local body. I needed to submit myself and my ministry to the prayerful guidance of the Lord's people. I had been making the mistake of *putting* myself in the position of authority without being submitted *to* authority. I was somewhat like a policeman trying to direct traffic without proper authorization from headquarters.

During the next six months I took two more trips from Frankfurt to Berlin, both of which confirmed that I needed to submit myself to a local body if I was to be protected by a spiritual covering.

The first trip took me eight hours, traveling alone by train. After our Monday night Bible study with American military personnel I caught a train from Walldorf to Frankfurt and took the midnight special to Berlin where I met Jeff. He and I would minister often together behind the curtain.

First we shared what God had done in each other's lives, then we visited Pastor Schmidt as soon as we got to East Berlin. The old man was excited to see us again, and he was more optimistic than ever that he might get to move to the west. The East German government doesn't care about older people anyway, and often they let them return to West Berlin just to keep from having to support them in their old age. It was wonderful to see him in such good spirits, and we prayed with him that his dream would be realized.

When Jeff and I took to the trains again for some witnessing, we devised a new plan. We did most of our riding during the time that the schools were letting out so the trains would be packed with young people. Then Jeff would stand at one end of the car and I would stand at the other. He would yell something to me in German about Jesus, and I would answer back. Soon everyone on the car would be quiet to hear what we were saying about Christ, and I would begin to preach. No pretense, just preaching.

Then we would start up conversations with individuals and we found, as always, that Communist kids are hungry to know the Gospel. After several hours of successful witnessing on the trains, Jeff and I visited the Russian military base that Pastor Schmidt had taken us to during an earlier visit. This was the one that I knew I would be coming back to one day.

We had Russian tracts and had been given a bunch of red Jesus stickers in Russian by a friend in West Germany. We passed out tracts and stuck the stickers anywhere they would stick. We had to be careful in passing out the tracts because very few people would take them for fear that they might be seen and punished.

The Russian military base was even tighter than the city of East Berlin, so we found ourselves often just planting a stack of tracts somewhere and watching the people come by and take them when they were sure the coast was clear. It was a blessing to see how quickly they disappeared.

At a restaurant we left over a hundred tracts and a bunch of Jesus stickers on a bench outside. Then we went in and ate, and by the time we got back outside, nearly all of the tracts and stickers had been taken.

We began to feel that people were watching us and might be following us, so we split up for awhile. Jeff was going to ride the trains for awhile and try to lose anyone who might be on his trail, and then he would visit Pastor Schmidt and meet me back at the base at 4:30.

As I walked around alone I began to feel a heavy burden for all the young people I saw. "God," I prayed, "is there a way that I could somehow share Jesus with these kids?" Just then I came upon a theater front where the children of some Russian soldiers were milling about.

I asked if any of them spoke German. Few did, but most could understand it. As I passed out tracts, more gathered. Since they spoke so little German, most of them assumed I was German in spite of my lack of fluency, and they began to ask lots of questions about Christ. Two kids stayed behind while the others walked on and continued to talk with me. They promised to take the *Four Spiritual Laws* booklet and pray about it. I was thrilled. God had answered my prayer.

I saw a girl and felt God leading me to talk with her. I handed her a tract and asked her if she knew Jesus. She said no. "Here," I said, "this is a present for you." I gave her a Bible.

"Oh, no," she said, pulling her hand away.

I said, "Yes, please take it. It's from the Lord." She took it. Without knowing the Russian language I knew I was having a ministry all the way to Russia because these Russian kids happened to be able to understand a little German. Praise the Lord.

Getting Bibles or any Christian literature into Russia is extremely difficult, and I could only pray that these kids would somehow be able to get these materials back during their visits.

When I met Jeff at 4:30 he was nervous because he felt someone was following him. We left quickly on the train and saw no one, but waited until the next day before we returned. He was thrilled to hear what had happened while he was away.

The next day at the base we noticed a little path leading to some woods. We saw a lot of Russian people walking down the path, so we followed them. It led to a housing project for military families and in the middle of the houses was a playground full of children and their parents.

We sat at one of the tables in the park and asked that God would bless us and help us to witness. When we opened our eyes, the answer came in the form of two young Russians who asked for cigarette money. We had none, but we asked if they had heard of the *Four Spiritual Laws*. We shared with them for an hour and found them very interested. They too had been taught in school that there was no God, but they continued to ask us questions about our personal experiences with God. "How do you know He's real?" they asked. "What differences did He make in you? Who is He, really?" Hungry hearts.

Later I said "Jesus loves you" in Russian to two women in the park, and they began screaming and drawing a crowd.

"What are we going to do, Jeff?" I yelled.

"Let's get out of here!" he said, and we took off running, each in a different direction. When we met up again he asked, "What in the world did you say to them?"

"Just 'Jesus loves you,'" I said.

He shook his head. "Wow, they're really upset. We'd better split."

As we headed toward the train I saw another group of young people. Jeff walked on but I stopped and handed them tracts and said, "Jesus loves you." As I moved on I noticed Jeff running on ahead and shouting at me.

"Come on! Come on!" I started running and looked behind me. Two young people were talking to two soldiers and were pointing at us. As we sprinted to the train we could see them running toward us. We skipped onto the train and prayed that it would begin rolling before they got there. It did.

To be safe we spent the rest of the day switching trains and walking through wooded areas back to town. We hid the rest of our literature and went across the border, more aware than ever that a covering was needed when you step out to serve God, especially as an alien.

I had planned one more trip to Berlin before the Communist Youth World Fest, and that would be the one which would help send me packing for the United States before even thinking of having a ministry without a covering.

Chapter Six

ALONE

Escaping from the soldiers at the Communist military base was the closest call I had had since visiting Europe, and it made me think twice about my family and our ministry. God began to speak to me about my willingness, or lack of it, to count the cost.

I had been threatened, run off the road, run out of town, held at gun point, shot at, arrested, and even jailed during my street ministry in the States, and I've always felt afterward that I had indeed been willing to die for my Lord. But, you know, dying is one thing. Living in prison is another. I can truthfully say that I would more willingly die for Christ than live for Him in prison.

In death my family would be left without a husband and father, but in the event of my imprisonment they would be subjected to constant questions, anxiety, and worry about my health, etc. And, of course, I would worry about them too. I decided that I would have to be more careful. I knew that I would have to become willing even to be imprisoned for my Lord, because in Europe that is more likely than martyrdom.

I was becoming more and more busy ministering in and around Frankfurt, and my German was improving. God showed me clearly that I needed to go back to America to submit myself to a local body who believed in our ministry and who would *send* us out.

I heard about a conference on the Holy Spirit being held in Switzerland under the direction of Jack Taylor, pastor of the First Baptist Church of Castle Hills, San Antonio, Texas. I knew of Taylor through his best-selling books on the Spirit-filled life, so I was anxious to attend.

At the conference I was strangely drawn to another San Antonio pastor and his wife, Mr. and Mrs. Bud Gardner of the Gateway Baptist Church. Neither said much during the entire conference, but when Brother Bud spoke, it seemed obvious that his thoughts were of God. His small church of 300 or so was in the process of being turned upside down, or right side up, for the glory of God.

During the last day of the conference I was led to share with Brother Bud my concern for our ministry and our need for a church which would be our covering and which would send us out by laying on hands and praying and fasting as was done in the thirteenth chapter of Acts. Brother Bud seemed genuinely excited about it, and I made tentative plans to move back to San Antonio and set up our headquarters there. We would maintain an active iron curtain ministry and would, of course, still plan heavily for the Communist Youth World Fest. But we would now have a home base, and the spiritual covering which God provides for those who are in submission to a local body of believers.

I was excited about the future because I knew that God would grant our ministry all authority in heaven and on earth if we were in the submissive position Jesus was in when He was on earth. That authority can literally tear down the gates of hell—and that was the type of authority we would need to combat Communism, atheism, and Satan behind the iron curtain.

During this time I had been writing to Fred Bishop, a pastor from southern Illinois who had ministered with us at the Democratic national convention in 1972. He was a bold witness with a good youth work going, and I was filling him in on our iron curtain work.

He felt the Lord leading him to help us in Europe, and I learned of this just before we planned to return to the States. We thought that perhaps Fred should spend some time with us in San Antonio preparing for the Youth Fest if God was actually calling Him to go too.

Meanwhile, I had to make one more trip to Berlin before we left for Texas. If I needed one more confirmation that we needed a covering, I got it on this trip.

Somehow Jeff got hung up on a short witnessing trip to Poland and was unable to meet me in East Berlin. I was loaded down with Bibles and tracts concealed all over my body. We had decided our policy on smuggling Christian literature behind the iron curtain would be as follows: we would never lie. If we were asked whether or not we had Bibles or tracts, we would say yes and would fill out any written documents likewise. We always pray that we will not be asked, and that if we are searched our materials will not be found. We have never been asked, and searches have never uncovered our literature.

I had Bibles stuffed in my pants, my shirt and everywhere else; tracts were up my sleeves and in my shoes. I was not asked or searched carefully, so I made it through without a problem. My plan was to go to a restaurant near the Russian military base and eat. Then I would go to the men's room and transfer all my literature from my person into a black case I carried. We had done it before, but now I was alone and a bit nervous. I noticed two Russian policemen sitting not far from me; all during the meal I wondered if they were suspicious of me.

I finished eating, and before paying, I followed a sign to the men's room. Trying to look nonchalant, I walked through the door and shut it quickly behind me before looking to see where I was. I wasn't in the men's room at all. I was in a laundry closet, and there was no handle on the inside of the door knob!

For an hour I sat there helplessly praying and asking God what I should do. There was no getting the door open, and I certainly didn't want to make any noise with those policemen close by. Maybe they had already seen me walk into the closet and had it surrounded. There was virtually nothing I could do but wait.

Suddenly the door opened before I could even get to my feet. A waitress was putting something away. I bolted upright and she gasped. Before she could say anything, and before I could even logically decide on a course of action, I just stepped past her, walked to the counter, slapped my money down, and kept moving. Everyone seemed to be staring and wondering what had happened, but I just kept walking right out the door and down the street. Whew! It seems funny now, but it wasn't then. That hour seemed like a week.

I had always depended on Jeff who knew some Russian and spoke fluent German. Now I was all by myself, and when I needed my poor German, it wouldn't come to me. My mind was clogged and I could hardly get simple sentences to make sense. I can't describe the loneliness I felt, it was almost physical. I knew I needed a covering and that without it (or at least a companion), that I wouldn't minister any more this trip. It would be too dangerous.

I wanted some more concrete details about the World Fest, but I didn't want to get into the same position Don, Ricky, and I had found ourselves in before. So I went through Alexanderplatz to the Evangelical Free Church, hoping that some Christian friends could tell me something.

No one in the church spoke anything but German or Russian, and my mind went blank. I couldn't say anything in German, I couldn't understand anything in German, I couldn't even *think* of anything in German. I seemed to have forgotten everything I had ever learned and I felt so lonely that I began to cry. I was devastated. It was as if I hadn't a friend in the world.

I bowed my head low as I sat in the pew and cried out, "O God, please, please do something for me." Praise God, as I sat there calling out to Him, I heard the faint strains of a chorus being sung in English. Two seats from me an old German lady was softly singing:

51

Loving you, loving you, Jesus I'm loving you more.

I asked her if she spoke English or if anyone spoke English there. She shook her head.

"Oh, but you must," I said.

Another little lady interrupted me in German. "No she does not speak English, she only speaks German. And even if you speak English, you should speak German in this church."

"But I just heard her speaking English," I said in perfect German. And then it hit me. I had completely understood the second lady's German! And I had answered her in fluent German!

I didn't have any more words than I had learned before, but God restored what I had learned and my faith was made strong through hearing that sweet English song. I knew He had been with me all the while.

I obtained more specifics about the World Fest and then hurried back to Frankfurt to prepare for our trip home. With not a possession to our names, we looked forward with great anticipation to the first real church "home" for our ministry. We would be back in just a few months for the Communist Youth World Fest.

Chapter Seven

REFUELING

I guess I'll never learn. Just when I think the Lord has taught me a good lesson in faith or patience, I prove that I need to be shown again. When the Lord impressed upon my heart that we should give away all of our appliances and furniture before we left Germany, I should have learned long before that His way was best.

But, no. I questioned it inwardly first. I thought of how much profit we could make by selling the stuff to some German people, then transferring the marks into dollars and making a killing because of the devaluation of the dollar at that time. I kept trying to rationalize that selling the stuff would be the best bet for us, but I could never get peace about it.

Trusting the Lord, perhaps without as much conviction as I would have liked, we made an unusual offer at our last Bible study session with the military people. "We have some things that the Lord has told us to give away," I said. "If you need anything, please talk to us after the meeting."

It was a beautiful experience. Every single item we had to give fit someone's specific need. In fact, every item had been on someone's prayer list. We had been used to answer many prayers and we were humbled by it. If that had been the only consequence or reason that God had in telling us to give these things away, we would have understood. But there were more blessings in store for us through it.

When we got back to the States we had only enough money to buy a small car. Besides that we had each other and our clothes—and our Bibles. I began to worry again. God had always provided just enough for us. We never had too much, but we always had enough. And yet my flesh is weak. When the money seems to be running low, my faith begins to waver. Praise God, He understands. Sometimes I think I must amuse Him, and I pray that my weakness doesn't disappoint him.

We visited both of our parents in Louisiana. Then before moving on to San Antonio, I had a week of meetings lined up in Sparta, Illinois. I had received requests for meetings from about a dozen churches, but I had felt led in prayer to accept only the Sparta invitation. The Lord had taught me that I didn't have to count on the love offerings of my meetings, but that I could always depend solely upon Him. He had always provided, whether I was speaking or not, yet our present situation made that harder and harder for me to remember. It just seemed that it might be a good idea to take a couple of weeks' worth of meetings to help financially. But the Lord said, "No, take just this one week." I would learn to trust Him yet.

What a blessed week of meetings we had in

Sparta! Many were saved. Many were filled with the Spirit. Many were delivered from the hands of Satan. Early in the week the Holy Spirit revealed to me that someone attending the meetings during the week would be a thief and would need to repent. On Thursday night, God spoke to my heart, telling me that this was the night the thief was in the service.

"There is someone in this service tonight who is in possession of stolen goods," I said. "You are going to have to make a confession. While our heads are bowed, I am going to ask you to come forward and get right with God."

Not one, but three people came down the aisle to confess their sin of stealing. We found later that several establishments in town reported that stolen property had been returned.

I was thrilled with how God was working, but my old sin of faltering faith kept creeping in. Everything was sailing along beautifully, yet I was worried about what we would do for money once we got to San Antonio and needed a place to stay, some household goods, and some food.

I knew the nightly offerings were to go to our ministry, but the pastor was not making a point of it to the congregation. He didn't say the usual, "Sammy's in a faith ministry," or "This is a love offering for the Tippits." All he said was, "We'll now have our evening offerings." I know how it appears for me to have worried about it, but it was a very real struggle to me. I felt bad that it even entered my mind, but I was thinking of my wife and child—almost as if I had forgotten that God was thinking of them (and me) too.

Of course, I didn't say anything to anybody about it, but I must admit I was sweating it. I didn't think there would be much to the week's offering since no specific appeal had been made.

On Sunday night the pastor handed me a check. "Our people have never given like this before," he said. The check was for over $1,000. I was thrilled, and rebuked. God had once again shown me that I must trust Him daily. Even in mundane money matters.

I'd like to say that that experience taught me the lesson once and for all. But it didn't. I have worried since, and always God proves Himself again and again. But I have never disobeyed His leading about not asking for money, though I might be tempted at times. I know there are many people who would give me what I ask for, but God demands that I trust Him, and not people. Each time it gets a little easier, and it's all part of my growth pattern.

When we got to San Antonio we used the money God had provided for furniture, appliances, rent, and food. And we immediately felt at home in the Gateway Baptist Church. One of the first things we noticed about the church was that there was no pretense about it. No one claimed that it was the perfect church or a super-spiritual church. It had its problems as does any body of believers. Some of the problems are very deep and very real, but God is at work.

Its location is uniquely strategic because it's so close to Lackland Air Force Base where military personnel from all over the world study different languages. A witness to a group of soldiers could have an international impact.

We felt good that we were going to submit ourselves and our ministry to this body of believers who were not just another church, but a people who would love us and care about us and pray for us. I was really impressed with the obvious depth of the prayer lives of many of the laymen. There were people here whose entire ministry was prayer. God had brought us into the midst of a band of real prayer warriors, and while we didn't know how long it would continue, we knew that for the time being, this was to be our church home and our spiritual covering. We were excited.

I had been corresponding with Fred Bishop in Illinois via letters and tapes, and he felt led of God that this was the time for him to resign as pastor of his church and move to San Antonio so we could begin planning for our ministry at the Communist Youth World Fest. It was a real act of faith for Fred and his wife to give up the security of a church situation and move to a place where virtually no one but us knew them. Fred would learn many hard lessons about the walk of faith during the next year.

Once the Bishops were settled in, Fred and I met every morning for prayer and Bible study. We would meet first with others from the church who were involved in full time ministries, then we would memorize Scripture passages and the *Four Spiritual Laws* in German so Fred would be able to help me at the Fest. He had had no exposure to the language, but I had finally become fairly fluent, even to the point where I would one day be mistaken for a German, by a German. Praise God!

Fred and I began translating some simple English choruses into German such as *He is Lord* and *God is So Good* and *Alleluia*. In teaching Fred to speak German, God helped me learn more and more too. Once we had the basics down, it was time for God to show us clearly the strategy for the Fest.

Chapter Eight

READY . . .

*"And while they were ministering to the Lord
and fasting, the Holy Spirit said, 'Set apart for
Me Barnabas and Saul for the work to which I
have called them.'*

*Then, when they had fasted and prayed and
laid their hands on them, they sent them away.*

. . . . and they also had John as their helper."
(Acts 13:2, 3, 5b, NAS)

*"Is this not the fast which I chose, to loosen
the bonds of wickedness, to undo the bands of
the yoke, and to let the oppressed go free, and
break every yoke?*

*"Is it not divide your bread with the hungry,
and bring the homeless poor into the house . . . ?*

*"Then your light will break out like the dawn,
and your recovery will speedily spring forth; and
your righteousness will go before you; the glory
of the Lord will be your rear guard."* (Isaiah
58:6, 7a, 8 NAS)

One morning Fred came by with the news that a brother at the church had given him two twenty-dollar bills, one for him and one for me. "He said that the Lord led him to do it," Fred explained. "He said that we would need it today."

Neither of us could think of anything we would need the money for that day, so we knelt to see what the Lord would have us do. In prayer we were impressed that we should rent a hotel room in town and just spend the day in prayer and fasting, totally away from any form of distraction.

As we spent the day in the hotel, God began to speak to our hearts and to indicate His will in regard to the Communist Youth World Fest. The first Scripture we were led to was Acts thirteen where Saul (Paul) and Barnabas were sent out as apostles and John Mark was commissioned as their helper. This was the first clue I had received as to the number of ministers who would go from the States to the Fest.

We felt led that my task would be similar to that of Paul's in preaching and proclaiming the Gospel. Fred's was to be as Barnabas's ministry. And Fred Starkweather, a young man who had come to Christ through Fred Bishop's ministry, was to be our John Mark.

We were thrilled with the Scripture God had given us, but something blew my mind. God seemed to be clearly saying that I was to preach publicly at the Fest! That was impossible. Up to that time I had assumed that ours would be an individual ministry, sharing the *Four Spiritual Laws* with people at the Fest. I didn't see how I could possibly preach to 100,000 Communists without getting hassled or arrested.

I continued to wonder whether God could actually be calling me to do that, but the Spirit impressed it heavily upon my heart. "OK, Lord," I said finally. "If that's what You want me to do, I'll do it. But, how?"

The Isaiah passage He led me to just thrilled my heart. He was promising to loosen the bands of wickedness and to let the oppressed go free! God was going to bless us in a way we could not even imagine. He was going to pour out His Spirit and do a tremendous work.

He promised that He would use us to break the bread of life and divide it to the hungry multitude if we would simply obey and trust Him, no matter how impossible His direction might seem. My whole being throbbed with wonder at the leading to preach at the Fest, but the last verse in the Isaiah passage sealed it for me. " . . . the glory of the Lord shall be thy rear guard." Praise His name!

How could the gates of hell prevail against us? How could anyone harm us if the glory of God was our protector? We spent the rest of the day fasting and praising God for His direction.

It was June, 1973, and we were to leave in about a month and a half for Germany. I was certain that we were ready to go except for last minute Bible studying, memorization, and brushing up on the language. But it turned out that God had yet another lesson for me.

With so little time left Tex, Davey, and I all came down with one form or another of the flu, a virus, colds, you name it. I couldn't understand it. Here I was sold out, dedicated, obedient, ready to go, and eager. And now this. It didn't make sense. If one of us wasn't sick, the other two were. Every time you turned around, one of us was flat on his back.

I spent a lot of time in soul-searching prayer, begging God to indicate what was wrong and beseeching Him to heal us in time to minister at the Fest to people who may never get another chance to hear His Word.

A brother from the church came over one evening to pray for us. He and his wife were in the habit of praying with Tex and me regularly every week. We had a lot in common. They were about our age, and had a young son too. When he prayed this night, though, he prayed with such compassion that I realized he'd have gladly taken our sicknesses upon himself, if that were possible.

When I told Fred Bishop about my friend's compassionate prayer, we decided he knew something about intercessory prayer that we *didn't* know. Taking a pad of paper, some pencils, and our Bibles, we went to visit him.

"Take the Word and teach us," we said. That night we learned that an intercessor is a bit different from a regular prayer warrior. An intercessor not only identifies with the problem of the person he's praying for, but he is willing to take that burden upon himself. The greatest example of intercession, of course, was Jesus, who "knew no sin," yet "became sin for us." On the cross He took our sin upon Himself that we might be set free. It was a heavy truth to know that now we can enter into the suffering of Christ on the cross when we are willing to take the problems of others upon ourselves.

It was an important lesson for me to learn before we went to the Fest because it revolutionized my prayer life. God spoke to my heart and showed me how I had been praying for months about the lives I wanted to see changed and the souls I wanted to see saved for God's glory. But was I willing to face the persecution that these people would face as a result of the decisions they would make?

In a short time, Tex, Davey, and I were set free from our illnesses. But now I had mixed feelings about the trip. On the one hand, I knew God had promised to work a spiritual miracle at the Fest. But now the question remained, was I willing to pay the price? Would I be willing to go to prison for any one or all of the people He would draw unto Himself through my ministry? That was a tough question, and I battled with it.

I was going to preach Christ and hold Him up so that men would be drawn to Him. I would be asking them, indeed exhorting them to sacrifice perhaps even their freedom to follow Him, regardless of the cost. Would I pay the same price? They would likely go to prison, many of them. "If you're going to ask them to do that," God said to my heart, "you must be willing to intercede for them."

That was not easy. It would be easier for me to die than to face a lifetime in prison. Yet that was what God was asking. It was as if He were trying to find out how serious I was about this whole scene.

Was I in it for the glory of marching into the World Fest and being able to say that I preached there? Was I on some spiritual high or ego trip? Was I into a two-bit witnessing crusade, or was I ready to lay my freedom on the line for Christ?

I was being taught a hard lesson. God was showing me that this ministry was His and not mine. It was His idea and not mine. The success would be His and not mine. If I wanted to play in this league, with this much at stake, and if I wanted to involve myself in a ministry at this level, then I had better get myself in gear and get close to Christ. And that would mean joining in the fellowship of the sufferings.

Was I ready? I searched my soul. In the flesh Sammy Tippit was not ready to give up his freedom for anything or anyone. But I wanted to be obedient. I wanted to serve Christ. I loved Him and wanted to share Him. I wanted more than anything to say that I would do so at any cost. I knew that only He would be so perfect in His love as to give Himself for lost souls, so I prayed that He would give me that supernatural love. I knew it was not a part of my natural self, so it would have to come from Him.

I also knew that it was no game. If I prayed for souls, adding to my prayer the fact that I was willing to go to prison for them, there was a real possibility (and surely no insurance against it) that God would require me to do just that. He is not in the business of providing a cozy life for Sam and Tex. He's in the business of drawing men unto Himself. If I wanted a part of that ministry, I had to count the cost.

God filled me with His supernatural love so that I could honestly pray that I would be willing to go to prison for any and all converts behind the Curtain. It was not just spiritual exercise. It was ominous. Fred Bishop, Fred Starkweather, and I made out wills and took care of arrangements in the event that we would never return.

At worst, we would be imprisoned. Or we could be killed. At best, we would return. It was almost time to go.

Chapter Nine

SET . . .

While I had had a busy ministry in the past in the northern midwest states, I was virtually a stranger in Texas. So few churches were aware of me down there that the only speaking invitations I received were coming from the Illinois area. I didn't feel right about leaving Tex and Davey, so several weeks went by without my having a chance to preach.

Of course I missed this spiritual outlet, and I longed to be used of God. But a bigger problem arose. You guessed it: I began to worry again about how God would provide the money for us to get to the World Fest if I weren't out preaching. My vision is so short and I limit my Lord so much that I marvel at His patience.

I just kept trusting and obeying Him, but I was also starting to sweat it. One reason was that we were one week from departure date and we were flat busted. I mean flat. Though we had deposited some money with the travel agency, it would take at least $1,100 more to get us to the World Fest—and I didn't have it.

I hadn't forgotten the promise of God that He would bless my public speaking at the Fest, so I knew we were definitely supposed to go. I began to wonder if I wasn't being led to borrow the money. Perhaps it was my pride over never having borrowed that was keeping me from it. I hit Fred Bishop with the idea.

"I don't believe that, Sam. I don't believe God would have you borrow the money," he said.

"But I'm willing to borrow," I said. "I've been in a faith ministry for a long time, but I'm willing to admit my lack of faith or anything necessary to raise the money to go. God has directed us to go, and we must obey."

"I don't believe God would have you borrow it," Fred repeated. "If He has called us to go, He'll provide." We prayed that He would.

Every last cent had gone into buying plane tickets and we had nothing left in our bank accounts. There was no pocket change, nothing stashed away in the cookie jar . . . nothing. The gas gauge of my car was on empty. And we still needed the $1,100.

An evangelist friend, David Stockwell, asked me to share my testimony at a big city-wide crusade he was having in a football stadium seventy miles north of San Antonio. He would then fly me on to Fort Worth in his own small plane so I could speak to the seminary class of Dr. Roy Fish at Southwestern Baptist Theological Seminary the next day. I looked forward to these two chances to share, but I didn't even have the money for gas to get me to David's meeting that evening.

Brother Bud, our pastor, invited Fred and me to a ministerial luncheon that day, so we went, not knowing how we would pay for our meal. God laid it on Brother Bud's heart to pay for us, though he was unaware of our plight. After we had eaten, a couple of men from the Billy Graham Evangelistic Association spoke briefly to the group. I had met one of them a few years before and wondered if he would remember me.

On his way out, without having said hello or anything, he reached over and shook hands with me, pressing a five-dollar bill into my palm. "Praise the Lord, it's good to see you again," he said.

Praise God, that gave us enough money to put two dollars' worth of gas in the car and three dollars for supper before the meeting. That night in the restaurant, as I thanked God for providing, I guess I waxed a little loud, as I usually do.

(When we were new in San Antonio, Tex and I were out to eat in a restaurant with Brother Bud and his family, and Bud called on me to pray. Their family was used to praying over their meals regardless where they were, of course, but I guess my volume freaked out his son. He told me later that everyone in the restaurant bowed their heads when I prayed because they thought I was leading for everyone!)

Anyway, when I finished praying in the restaurant this night, a man approached us. "I'm a Lutheran pastor on vacation from Missouri," he said. "God touched me as you were praying, and I think we need more young men who will stand for Jesus Christ. Allow me the privilege of paying for your meals." Praise the Lord! I was beginning to see that, once again as always, God will take care of His own. There we were, paupers, eating as children of the King.

That night at David's crusade I was on cloud nine. "A lot of people talk about what God did for them five years ago when they were saved," I told the crowd. "Or when they were filled with the Spirit four months ago. But I'm just thrilled that I can stand up here and tell you what God has done for me this very day!" I was excited and bubbling all over as I shared the little ways in which God had provided. His Spirit is still as fresh and real to me today as it was when I became a Christian as a senior in high school in 1965.

Immediately after my testimony, and before he spoke the evening message, David told me that we would have to leave the meeting quickly and not stand around talking to people if we were to get to the airport and on to Fort Worth in time. I didn't like that idea much, but it was his service and I was in submission to him. I generally like to fellowship and minister, but I agreed that we were pressed for time.

At the end of the meeting, people came running up to talk and pray with me. I ministered quickly to a few and chatted briefly with others. Then as I started to leave I noticed that several were stuffing money into my pockets. When I finally got to the car I said, "Fred, you're not going to believe this."

"What?"

I started pulling bills and change out of my pockets which totaled almost seventy dollars. We praised the Lord.

David had to land for refueling in Waco on our way to Fort Worth, and the Lord led me to stay by the plane and pray while David and Fred were witnessing inside the terminal. I could feel as I prayed that God was working, and I would find out later that two people received Christ that night at the airport. As I prayed, I thanked God for letting me see His power and feel the presence of His Holy Spirit.

By the outpouring of the love of God's people three different times that day I was able to see that God was still in command. I knew He had called me apart to preach the Gospel and that He would bless and provide. I wept as I praised Him for anointing me and having His hand on me and revealing Himself to me.

We flew on to Fort Worth and stayed in David's home. Though he was a student at the seminary, yet he carried on a full-time evangelistic preaching ministry. The next morning I spoke in Dr. Fish's class of about 150, sharing again how God had provided and how we had learned that the only successful power in witnessing comes directly from the Holy Spirit. Our street ministering had always been fruitless when we went on our own fleshly power, but when we let the Spirit take over, God blessed.

As I spoke I could see that God was working in the class. People were moved as I told how God had given us power and authority over demons and Satan worshippers on the streets. When I finished, Dr. Fish said, "Any of you who must leave for other classes may go. But, for me, and anyone else who would like, let's gather 'round the front here and pray with Sammy." It was a blessed experience. Many of the students confessed sin and got right with God right there in the classroom.

One girl came to me and said she had heard

me preach more than a year before. "I didn't do it then," she said, "but I must do it now." She handed me a check for $100. God had told her to do that the first time she heard me preach, and she had been battling it ever since.

David came to me also and gave me a check for $250. I was overwhelmed. He said God had laid it on his heart. When he, Dr. Fish, Fred and I went with some of the students to a nearby restaurant for a bite, we were just overflowing with the goodness of God. We joined hands around the table and softly sang, *God is so good, God is so good, God is so good, He's so good to me.* And I'll tell you what: we knew it; and we meant it!

On Sunday evening (the night before we were to leave for Germany), I was invited to ride with a member of the First Baptist Church of Castle Hills when he went to the airport to pick up Haralan Popov, author of *Tortured For His Faith.* I was thrilled that I might get the chance to just meet and talk with him. Perhaps he could give me some idea of what to expect from an overt ministry behind the iron curtain.

At the airport we learned that Popov's flight had been delayed. He was to speak that night at Castle Hills, but a second announcement of delay sent my friend to be alone for prayer. When he returned he said that God had told him that the reason Popov was late was because I was supposed to speak.

"Are you sure?" I asked.

"Yeah, I'm sure."

The only administrative person I knew at Castle Hills was Pastor Jack Taylor, and he was out of town.

"What will the people in charge say?" I asked

my friend. Without answering, he called the church and talked to the associate pastor who was already waiting on the platform.

"God told you *who's* supposed to speak?"

"Sammy Tippit."

"Who?"

"Sammy Tippit."

"Well, I don't know—all right, bring him up quickly."

There were over a thousand people in the service that night, excited about hearing Haralan Popov. I was introduced as someone with something to share until Popov's plane arrived. I spoke for just twenty minutes, sharing what God had told us to do at the Communist Fest and what He had done for us in recent days. The Spirit touched people's hearts and they were burdened to pray for us.

The associate pastor said, "I think we should get on our faces before God and pray for this upcoming ministry." And these were praying people. They didn't simply sit, nor did they stand and bow their heads. They turned and knelt, the whole throng. It was a blessed sight as they called upon the Lord. As the last *Amen* was heard, Haralan Popov walked in. It was perfect.

They took an offering, had some special music, and then he spoke for almost an hour, blessing our hearts. When he was finished, another offering was taken for Brother Popov, making it even more incredible later when people once again began stuffing my pockets with money. After two offerings had been taken, these people were still anxious to give. I just praised the Lord for the people who came and hugged me and promised to pray for us.

One brother who had done some work overseas

with Arthur Blessitt came and gave me 20,000 Jesus stickers printed in Russian.

When I got home I had almost forgotten about the money. I began telling Tex of all the people who had promised to pray and about the prayer chapel at the church in which someone is praying constantly around the clock. "Praise the Lord," she said. "There are certainly going to be a lot of people praying for us."

"There sure are," I agreed. "And let me show you something else." I started pulling wads of money out of my pockets and found that God's people had given us $350. Money had come through the mail during the week as well, so we had a total of $1,000 the night before we were to leave, just $100 short of what I had figured we would need. I had not a doubt in the world that God would provide.

Chapter Ten

GO . . .

Our plans were to get a good, long night's sleep, rising at 9:00 A.M. and leaving at 11:00 by car. Fred Bishop had taken his family to Illinois where they would wait for him with friends. Fred was going to then fly to Nashville, Tennessee, with Fred Starkweather, where I would pick them up at the airport. We would then drive on together to New York and begin our flight to Germany.

Our schedule was interrupted a bit by a phone call at seven in the morning. The man introduced himself as a stranger who had heard me speak the night before at the Castle Hills Church. "The Lord laid it on my heart to talk with you this morning. Could you come by the union stockyards in town?"

"Well, not really," I said. "We're on a tight schedule because we have to be in Nashville late today."

"It won't take but five minutes, and I really need to talk to you," he said. I agreed, and we left a bit early.

At the stockyards this brother said, "All I have to say is that the Lord laid it on my heart to give you this." He handed me two fifty-dollar bills. Praise the name of Jesus. God had once again used one of His own to meet our needs. It was the last hundred dollars we needed, right to the penny.

Tex and I drove on with renewed excitement, knowing that God had a really heavy trip in store for us. The twelve-hour trip to Nashville was better than we expected because the Lord allowed Davey, not yet two years old by then, to have a good time. Davey is not always the best long-distance traveler, especially by car. But this time he was not only quiet, but he actually had fun. It was another blessing from God. One we needed on the first leg of a long journey.

We packed all the luggage on the top. Fred and Fred (as I came to call them throughout the trip) piled in with us. We traded off sleeping and driving and made a stop of a few days in Radford, Virginia. Lloyd Cole, his wife, and son had a street ministry there. Lloyd had been my associate director of *God's Love in Action* in Chicago, and it was great to see him again. I was able to speak at a couple of places, and held a rally and a march where we saw souls saved. To me it was just another confirmation that this entire trip was of God. It was great encouragement to us that He would begin giving us fruit even as we traveled to our ultimate assignment.

After catching up on our sleep during the stay with Lloyd and his wife, we began the last leg of our journey refreshed and in good spirits. We were so eager to get on that plane from Kennedy International and get going.

We hit New York City during the afternoon rush hour, and only a miracle got us to the airport in time for our plane. We made it through the traffic in an hour, and we still aren't sure how.

At the airport Tex washed her hair in the ladies' room while Fred and Fred sought out some Germans to help them with their "pronunciation of this little pamphlet" (the *Four Spiritual Laws*—it gave them a perfect witnessing opportunity).

Tex put her watch down while she washed her hair. It was stolen. Fred and Fred and I all had watches, but they'd quit running a few weeks before, so Tex's was the last watch between us. I believe God was trying to tell us that we would have to get our minds off mundane things like schedules, clocks, and calendars. We were to simply trust and follow Him in everything.

By the time we had made our connecting flights and wound up in Germany, Fred and Fred were wiped out. We all were, but it was so good to be back in Germany that I was keyed up. God would show me in the next few days that He would continue to bless us. I would run into several people who had grown closer to Christ through our previous German ministry.

Bob and Patty Holcomb, a couple about our age who had grown in the Lord through our ministry to the American military there, had fixed up their home near Walldorf to accommodate Tex, Davey, and me, as well as Fred and Fred. They had really gone all out to give us the best accommodations, and our comfort there was another blessing of the trip.

We spent three or four days there just resting

74

up before heading toward Berlin, and I was able to minister to different groups and do some preaching. In a shopping center I ran into a young German whom I had led to the Lord during our very first trip to Germany.

A couple of nights later, Fred and Fred and I were witnessing at the train station when a couple of guys overheard me talking about Jesus. "Sammy, Sammy," one said. I looked and who should it be but another guy I had led to Christ during our previous trip. We had a great reunion and enjoyed fellowshipping.

We were ministering one night in the nightclub district (which incidentally makes American nightclubs look like Sunday school picnics) and saw two come to Christ and were able to minister to a couple of American military personnel. At the train station on the way back a guy approached me. "I know you," he said. "You marched across Germany with a cross and I heard you preach at some rallies in Berlin."

He had been under conviction since that time, and while he did not receive Christ at the rallies, nor at the train station that night, I know he was on the verge and I pray that he has by now trusted Christ as his Savior.

The World Fest was just a few days off and I was getting eager. We would be moving on to Berlin where we would stay during the Fest and would be crossing the border every day to minister. Before we left for Berlin, I was to speak to the body of believers we had started, made up of the American military. Just before I spoke, I heard the news.

The Communists had decided to close the borders to the World Fest. No westerners would be allowed.

Chapter Eleven

ATTACKED ATTACKED,
AND ATTACKED

We had prepared for months and months and had seen God provide the money for us to travel all the way from America for the Communist Youth World Fest, and now the borders were to be closed to all but the registered delegates. Satan had begun to attack already. In a matter of hours he would hurl woes my way in a frantic attempt to discourage us. But he would not succeed.

I spoke that night to the body of believers about the new truth I had learned on intercessory prayer. Was I worried about the border closing? No, because God had given us a Scripture in prayer earlier in the day.

As we poured out our hearts to Him concerning

the news, He had impressed upon us to read Revelation 3:8. Praise God! We couldn't have gotten a clearer promise. "I know your deeds. Behold, I have put before you an open door which no one can shut, because you have a little power, and have kept My word, and have not denied My name."

I was rebuked, too. The Lord seemed to demand of me, "Are you going to trust the Communists or are you going to trust Me?"

"I am going to trust you, Lord." Why would He have led this far if He weren't going to get us in? And why the clear promise that I would preach publicly at the Fest if we were to be kept away? Why the leading about my ministry being as Paul's, Fred Bishops's as Barnabas's, and Fred Starkweather's as John Mark's? God impressed upon us that when He opens a door, we don't have to care what any puny earthly government says, or what the radio or television or newspapers say. All we have to concern ourselves with is the fact that God said the doors would be open. And so they would.

Of course, we still didn't know how God would get us in. We simply trusted that He would. Perhaps He wanted us to fly to Poland and come in another way. Or, perhaps—well, we just didn't know. After the meeting we caught the midnight special train to Berlin, leaving Tex and Davey in Frankfurt until we knew what the specific strategy would be. Just Fred and Fred and I would be going to the Fest anyway. Tex would remain in West Berlin during those few days, but until then we thought it best if she waited in Frankfurt.

We arrived in Berlin the next morning and we were whipped. Our luggage was heavy and we had hardly slept at all on the trip. We made our way to a cabin which had been arranged for us in a beautiful place on the river called Wansee. We spent the day resting up and praying, and that evening I decided to take Fred and Fred to the wall. Satan was about to make a direct attack.

The wall hit me with the same intensity as always, and it was, of course, a new experience for Fred and Fred. As we stood there weeping and praying before God, Fred noticed a man staggering up the steps overlooking Checkpoint Charlie.

"He looks blind," Fred said. "Maybe we should help him."

As the man reached the top he bumped into me and I could see from his eyes that he was not blind. The Holy Spirit said clearly to me, "Get away. Get away from this man." I backed away but the man kept moving toward me, talking in German. The Spirit told me not to talk with him. "My German is not very good," I said quickly. "I really can't talk with you."

But the man (whom we nicknamed Checkpoint Charlie) persisted. I ignored him and he left, staggering down the steps again. He wasn't gone, though. We noticed him waiting for us at the bottom. We went the other way, deciding to ask the American soldiers at the border if they knew anything more about the decision concerning the Fest being open to westerners.

As we headed toward the guards (by now it was about midnight), I noticed a woman walking a dog about a half block away. She loosened the leash and said something to the dog in German. The dog charged away from her and past several people, snarling and growling savagely. I could tell immediately that the dog was heading straight for me. He passed several people on the street and even ignored Fred and Fred, barking and leaping toward my face as I back-pedaled to keep from getting bit.

Fred and Fred immediately fell to their knees, pleading the blood of Jesus over me and commanding the dog in the name of Jesus to retreat. It did. I was badly shaken. The dog had made a direct attack at me, and for no reason! I stood there shaking my head when suddenly "Checkpoint Charlie" approached and said cryptically, in German, "How would you like to go across the border with that dog?"

I was totally grossed out. It was like a weird nightmare. I felt the presence of Satan. We left Charlie and prayed the blood of Jesus would be our covering as we walked. We asked the guards if they had heard anything about the border closing and they said that the decision had been reversed. Praise God! He had opened the doors as He had promised. Satan had been trying to keep us from getting that information.

"We are advising Americans not to go over anyway," one of the guards said. "It could be very dangerous." How well we knew that! It wouldn't keep us away though. We were going under the authority of a higher power, and the glory of the Lord would be our rear guard.

On the train back to Wansee we agreed that it was good to be away from Checkpoint Charlie and the dog and everything else. Just then we noticed a man in the same car: Charlie! We could hardly believe it. At the next two stops we switched trains, only to find him on the same train both times. Finally, we had to get off the train and walk in and out of places downtown to lose him. We never saw him again, but I know it was part of Satan's warfare to spook us. It was really weird.

When we finally took our last train ride to Wansee I discovered that our evening hadn't been totally complete. I knew Satan had tried to cloud our minds, so I thought I should keep trying to witness, even though my mind had been blown with Charlie and the dog and everything. Seizing my first opportunity, I struck up a conversation with a nice looking woman in her late twenties.

She read a tract and seemed to be interested; I talked to her until it was time for us to go and she said she would like to talk more. I was praising God as she gave me her address, until she put her hand on my chest and said, "I'm very, very interested." I was grossed out again. I left her quickly and tore up the paper with her address on it. Dogs, weirdos, and now sex. Satan had attacked in so many ways in just a few hours, I was nearly spent.

Fred and Fred and I all slept in the same room in the cabin that night, even though there were plenty of rooms for each of us. We knew there was safety, even spiritually, in numbers, so we claimed the blood of Christ, praised God, and slept in the presence and under the protection of the Holy Spirit. The glory of God was our rear guard.

We knew one thing for sure. Satan was only so active because he was afraid of the moving of the hand of God. Surely, the Lord must have something heavy for us waiting at the Communist Youth World Fest.

Chapter Twelve

DRY RUN

Two days before the Fest we woke up excited. This was the day that we would make a dry run, giving Fred and Fred the experience of crossing the border, checking out the scene, and getting a feel for the whole area.

I called Tex and told her that the borders would be open to daily visits from West Berlin, and that she should come to Wansee where she could stay and be our daily prayer warrior. We had decided that if any of us were arrested at the Fest, the others would get the word to Tex so she could get the ball rolling to inform Christians in the States. We had a whole network set up so that within hours many of the news media in the Christian world would know that a Christian had been imprisoned by the communists.

Excitement was so high over the upcoming Fest that the delegates had already started to flood the city. Here the affair was actually two full days away, yet it took us well over an hour to bet across the border due to the crowds.

Though the tension of standing in line and waiting was exhausting, the crowds were really a blessing in disguise. The three of us were laden down with tracts, and we had some of the 20,000 Russian Jesus stickers stuffed in our shirts, pants, shoes, and jackets. Because of the number of people crossing, the border guards were very lax, and we were processed quickly once our turns came up. Our passports were checked and okayed, then we were given our twenty-four-hour visas for passage into East Berlin.

First I took Fred and Fred to the Russian military base where Jeff and I had done so much witnessing. They enjoyed the stories of how we had left tracts and stickers in obvious places and had then watched as people took them one by one. So we tried it again, and it worked. There's something really exciting about helping these military families in their search for something outside a political ideology. Since we didn't hand them the literature personally, and since they checked first to see that no one was watching, there was little threat to them in just lifting a tract and getting the Gospel.

In the park near the housing portion of the base we noticed that the bushes were unusual. The roots or trunks were thick, but the foliage spread out from the center and hung down, leaving a completely hidden open space near the trunk. We stacked some tracts and stickers beneath these bushes for later use and decided that this might be a good spot to store the bulk of our literature for the World Fest.

We did some one-on-one witnessing at the military base, then I took Fred and Fred to Alex-anderplatz which was to be the center of evening activities at the Fest. Everywhere we walked we stuck the Russian *Jesus Loves You* stickers on anything and everything. Of course, many of the delegates would be from Russia, and most of the others would be familiar with the language. Everywhere they looked they would be getting the message of the love of Christ.

Alexanderplatz was bustling with people. Plain-clothes policemen, trying to look inconspicuous, were the most obvious men around. With hands folded, standing in one spot for long periods, wearing conservative suits, and watching everything, they were embarrassingly obvious. We were impressed, however, with their number. They were everywhere.

The Fest originators were setting up the huge sound system which would boom the communist teachings to the hundreds of thousands of people who would make their way through Alexander-platz during the Fest. Propaganda literature was already being distributed, and estimates were that a half million people would visit the Fest daily and 100,000 delegates would fill Alexander-platz nightly. There seemed to be an air of expectancy surrounding everything and everyone connected with the Fest. But no one could have been more excited and anxious than we were. We had something no one else had. And we were going to share it.

We spent much of the next day in prayer back at Wansee. I was scheduled to speak that night at a church in West Berlin while Fred and Fred were teaming up on another venture. Fred Bishop would stay at the cabin and pray while Fred Starkweather crossed the border once more with gobs of Christian literature. He was going to hide the stuff in the bushes at the military base so we could get it quickly as we needed it at the Fest.

Satan went to work that evening. While I was speaking in West Berlin, Fred Bishop was hit with fear and doubt as he prayed for Fred Starkweather. Satan put into his mind the fear that the other Fred was going to be caught and imprisoned, and that it would be Fred Bishop's fault for bringing him to Europe. Fred Starkweather was gone even longer than I was, so these doubts and fears had really begun to work on Fred Bishop. Every minute longer that Fred Starkweather was gone, Fred Bishop was more convinced that it was his fault that Fred was going to spend years in prison.

Meanwhile, things weren't going entirely smoothly for Fred Starkweather. He had cleared the border easily, though again the pre-Fest crowds caused delay. After getting through that bottleneck, he eagerly made his way to the park near the military base and hid the literature in the bushes—only to notice as he rose to leave that a young Russian boy had been watching him. He didn't know what the consequences would be. The boy could tell someone who might find the literature and benefit from it, or he could tell the authorities and it would be confiscated, or he could just forget it, or—the possibilities were endless.

At the church where I was speaking, some of the brothers brought to my attention a Communist women's magazine which was being circulated in the area. One of the articles warned the delegates that the "Jesus People" would be coming to the Fest, and that they should be ready with their arguments. The pastor said he was glad we were going because he'd hate to see us disappoint the Communists.

The delegates had been trained carefully on how to argue with Christians. In a way this excited me because we knew that they considered us a bona fide threat, but on the other hand, we knew there would be no undercover work. They would be watching for us, indeed looking for us.

When I got back to our cabin from the church, Fred Bishop was a wreck. He just knew that Fred Starkweather had been caught and would be imprisoned. I tried to assure him that there was really very little danger of that at this point, but we both felt a lot better when Fred returned, though we were concerned about the boy who had seen him.

One thing I was beginning to see during these last few days before the Fest was that the communists didn't fear actual anti-Communistic stands or ideas. These were easy for them to stand against. They had all the answers, and their answers at least *sounded* logical. What they feared was someone with an alternative, someone who would forget trying to argue against their system in favor of presenting an alternative—like Jesus Christ. They truly feared a Jesus movement, an outpouring of the Spirit of God.

We had to come to the point where we realized that this was not political warfare. The solution to the problems of these people was not an anti-Communist crusade, even though we were totally aware of the deficiencies of their ideas. The solution was an outpouring of the Holy Spirit, because the Bible says that we wrestle not with flesh and blood but against powers and principalities.

It was spiritual warfare. If we tried to attack on a physical level, battling political systems, we would be stalemated. Our weapons were to be prayer and witnessing and preaching, in the boldness of the Spirit.

It was great to see Jeff again. He and a friend, Skip (not his real name), were excited to hear our plans for the Fest, and they wanted to get involved too. Jeff spoke Russian and German and played the guitar, things that would be real assets in our Fest ministry. Jeff and Skip would be joining us after the first two days of the Fest.

The Fest was just one full day away. And until Jeff and Skip joined us, there would just be Fred and Fred and Sammy—three behind the curtain.

Chapter Thirteen

THE DAY BEFORE

What an air of expectancy washed over the city of Berlin the day before the Communist Youth World Fest! Hundreds of thousands of the elite Communist young people from all over the world were pouring into the city, and the news media were filled with stories of the activities to come.

It was a perfect day. The sun was shining. The air was cool. The borders were jammed, and the city was geared up and ready for the Fest. I was anxious to see what God had in store for us. Somehow I knew that He would be giving us an idea of what to expect at the Fest when we crossed the border this day. This was to be one of the most important days of my life.

We spent some time at the lake that morning in prayer, fervently seeking the Lord. It was becoming obvious with every passing day that this ministry was much too big for us. Here were three foolish men who just wanted to trust God and obey Him. We were in over our heads and we knew it, but we believed that with God nothing is impossible. We wanted to completely die to ourselves, because we knew that the minute Fred, Fred, or Sammy tried to do anything for God in the flesh—especially at this mass meeting of atheistic minds—we would fall flat. There was simply nothing that we could accomplish here in the midst of 100,000 Communists unless we were dead to self and alive to the Holy Spirit.

We bubbled with excitement as we prayed. The Spirit seemed to be saying to our hearts, "God will do something in this city. He will pour forth the Life of His Son Jesus Christ on this place."

We thought the border had been crowded the day before! This day was unbelievable. We were sure that with the thousands trying to get in, the border guards would be even more lax than they had been. But we were wrong. We had stuffed our clothes with more tracts and stickers, assuming that there would be a cursory search and the usual passport and visa business.

As it developed, every fourth or fifth person was pulled from the line, taken to a back room, and searched thoroughly. The Fest hadn't even started yet and we were being forced to totally trust God. We prayed as the line inched forward that none of us would be chosen to be searched. "Lord," we prayed, "we're just trusting You to get us across." He did. The eyes of the border guard passed over us as he chose those who were to be searched.

The word was that the border checks would get stricter, not more lax, as the Fest began. We would have to deal with that later.

I knew that the city would be crowded, and that there would likely be a lot of activity, even a day before the Fest was to officially begin. But I confess I was not prepared for the sights that day. It was absolutely incredible. I had never seen so many people in one place at one time in my entire life. I just stood gaping. Thousands upon thousands upon thousands of young people were jammed into the main train station and hardly anyone could move. It was like a giant sardine can. But in spite of all that, various groups had come to demonstrate and they were determined to carry out their intentions.

The Free German Youth flooded like a blue wave over the whole scene. Other groups seemed to be huddled together. In one area, there was a demonstration of thousands of Italians against the imperialist United States. In another area, there was a crowd of happily singing Russians. It was the heaviest thing I have ever seen and it blew my mind. I was speechless.

When I say that every ten feet there was a uniformed policeman or soldier, I am not exaggerating. I mean it literally. It was a police state, and they covered the entire area. How ironic the term *Free German Youth* seemed to me when I saw all the military. I hadn't seen so many men in uniform anywhere, including Israel which was in the middle of a war!

As we inched our way through the crowd, hardly able to see each other, let alone stay together, I was struck with an overwhelming sense of defeat. This was not yet even the first day of the Fest. The crowds would get bigger! How could we possibly minister? And how could I possibly preach? My faith was small but I continued to trust the Lord. I knew it didn't have to be *possible* as long as He was in it.

We headed toward the Russian military base to stash away some more of our literature and to be sure that Fred Starkweather's original supply was still there. He waited at the train station for us for fear that he might be recognized from his first venture.

When we got to the park, we discovered that all of the literature Fred had stashed had been taken. Whoever the young boy was, he obviously had informed authorities. They would be watching for similar materials, and they would likely have some kind of description of Fred. We didn't know what they might try to do to stop us, but we left it in the Lord's hands.

The task seemed more ominous by the minute. I thought I had counted the cost when I learned about intercession in San Antonio. I had prayed that I would be willing even to go to prison for anyone who was converted at the Fest. I had prayed that very day that we would get rid of fleshly doubts, and yet already the combination of crowds and soldiers and defeat was blitzing me. I gave up trying to be prepared for every obstacle. There was no way to be ready for everything Satan was to throw our way expect to totally give it to God as we had done before. It would be a continual process. As more and more seemingly impossible situations arose, we would just pray, "Lord, it is in Your hands. We've counted the cost and we'll continue forward for You no matter what."

It was like walking briskly through a brick wall, blindly trusting that God would somehow open the way. We no longer had a choice. We had no alternative but to trust Him, because even if we wanted to try this mission on our own, we had already run out of ideas. There was nothing that we could do. I wouldn't say we were skeptical, but we sure knew that God would need to move in some mighty, mighty way to glorify Himself in this situation.

We still had this matter of hundreds of pieces of Christian literature and Jesus stickers. There was obviously nowhere to hide them, at least not on the Russian military base. So we felt led to start our witnessing and tract-passing campaign that very day. We weren't going to be reckless, but we *were* going to be fools for Christ. We would pass tracts and stick stickers until we were arrested or worse.

We rode the trains from station to station, passing tracts and stickers. Each car was so packed that we often had to stand, along with many of the other passengers. Finally our boldness grew and we began speaking loudly to each other about Jesus right in the middle of a packed train car. When the Communist young people would get quiet to hear what we were shouting about, I'd just take over and start preaching. Often we'd sing Christian choruses in German to get attention.

We boarded one train with three Russian soldiers. I stood debating with myself as to what we should attempt when they were standing right there. Would it be practical to get arrested and jailed even before the Fest began? It was a weird feeling. But then I realized that we were going to wind up witnessing and preaching in front of the military at the Fest anyway, so there was no sense waiting. There was no sense to *any* of this really, except that God had sent us, and we would obey Him.

91

I looked at Fred Bishop and he looked at me with no expression. The only words I knew in Russian were *Jesus loves you*. I said them to the soldiers and handed one a tract in Russian entitled *How to find Peace with God*. One of the soldiers said *Jesus loves you* back to me, and another patted me on the shoulder, saying something I didn't understand.

I didn't know what to make of it, though it was clear that they were just as puzzled by me. The one soldier read the tract and then showed it to his friends. When they got off the train, they waved and smiled. The Lord welled up inside me and I felt warmed by their receptivity, knowing that virtually anything could have happened. I'd had so much trouble with Russians in the past (like those screaming women in the military base and the soldiers who had chased Jeff and me to the train), that all I could say was, "Praise God. Thank you, Lord."

We headed back toward Alexanderplatz, distributing more and more literature as we went, and noticing also that the crowds kept getting bigger. With the many young people who filled the plaza came dozens more policemen and soldiers. There would be no leniency. Security would be tight. We prayed among ourselves again, asking that God show us how we were to minister in this massive prison block.

Not far away was Marx-Engles Platz where the huge statue of Karl Marx stands. We stood near the statue, noticing the concrete wall just below it. It seemed like a good place to stick the *Jesus loves you* stickers, and since no one was watching, we began sticking. We arranged several stickers in the shape of the cross. To our amazement, we glanced back as we walked away and saw the stickers glowing in the dark! It was unreal. We were some 200 yards away and we still could see that cross of stickers glowing red under the statue of Marx. We praised the Lord.

Another cross that would come to mean much to us at the Fest was one which reflected off the huge television tower in Alexanderplatz. The Germans are proud of this huge TV tower which can be seen for miles on both sides of the border. Strangely, though, the architect had designed it in such a way that the sun would reflect the shape of a cross on the tower during much of the day. The Communists had done many things to change the way the sunlight bounced off the tower, but St. Walter's Cross, as it came to be known, just kept shining. It was to become the banner under which we met as a body of believers during the Fest. Even in the midst of persecution we would be able to glance up and see the reflected cross and remember the cross of Jesus Christ and what He suffered for us. It would make our impossible mission seem more possible.

We returned to West Berlin and spent much of the evening in prayer. We saw no way that we would be able to preach publicly the next day at the Fest. All we had was the promise of God. But as we had learned and would continue to learn daily, the promise of God is all anyone needs.

Part Two

THE MISSION

Chapter Fourteen

DAY ONE: Autographs

The Communist Youth World Fest officially opened on a Sunday evening. It took us longer than ever to get across the border, but we were not searched. We could hardly believe that we were actually entering the Fest. Our day had finally come.

When we got to Alexanderplatz, the final torrent of young people had flooded into the area. I had thought I would never again see as many people as I had seen the day before, but this night proved me wrong. As far as the eye could see to the north, south, east, and west, there was nothing but young people, policemen, and soldiers. Even from the second and third floor windows of the surrounding buildings you couldn't see the ends of the throng.

This night my reaction was a bit different than it had been previously, however. I was not so overwhelmed with the impossibility of ministering in such a situation (though I was still wondering how in the world . . .) as I was with the depth of the burden God gave me. Suddenly this wasn't just a massive crowd of young people; it was tens of thousands of lost individuals who needed Jesus.

My heart just ripped apart. My eyes bulged as I tried to take it all in. Silently we prayed, "Lord, there are just three of us. How can we reach these kids? How can we do it?"

I prayed, "Lord, You told me to preach. How? Where? When?" Then I realized something. There would *never* be an opportune time to try to preach in this situation, so there was no sense waiting for one.

Small bands of young people from all over the world were in clusters doing their own things. The Free German Youth were sprawled in the grass, singing and playing guitars. A group of Hungarians drew a crowd with a folk song and dance. Other kids of other nationalities drew crowds of onlookers by performing skits. The atmosphere was one of a giant rock festival, except for all the security.

My heart went out to the young people, and suddenly my eyes fell on a young man. He was wearing a Jesus sticker! Could it be? A Christian Communist? I asked him in German, "Are you a Christian?"

"Oh, no. I found this sticker on the ground."

As I shared with him what his sticker meant (it read *One Way: Jesus*), a friend joined him and I witnessed to them for several minutes. I shared the *Four Spiritual Laws*. It didn't surprise me to hear the usual Communist's response, "Oh, I have been taught in school that there is no God. But what you are talking about is very interesting to me and I would like to hear more."

What did surprise me, though, was that our conversation seemed to be drawing a crowd. It was a big deal at the Fest to get the autograph of a foreigner, and I guess everyone within ear-shot could tell easily that my German was heavily influenced by my American heritage. The crowd gathered in the hope of getting the autograph of someone from the States. The young people all wore scarves, on which they collected the autographs of kids from the various countries.

The Lord gave us an idea as the kids asked us to sign their kerchiefs. I pulled Fred and Fred close and told Fred Bishop to write in German, "God loves you and has a wonderful plan for your life," before signing his name. Fred Starkweather would write, "Man's sin has separated him from this plan," and then sign his name. And before signing my name, I would write that Jesus was the only way to bridge the gap left by sin, along with a note of how to receive him.

We would explain the plan of salvation to any who were curious about what we'd written, but even if they didn't ask, we knew that before they slept that night they would likely read the names and notes on their scarves. We must have signed between two and three hundred scarves that night alone. The Lord had opened a great and ingenious avenue for witness.

I felt the presence of God upon us and I became more and more bold as we witnessed with various kids. I couldn't forget God's command to preach and His promise that His glory would be my rear guard. The time had come. There would be plenty of opportunities to share one-to-one. I had been called to preach.

I grabbed Fred Bishop and said, "Fred, stand here and don't say a word, no matter what I do."

"What do you mean? What're you gonna do?"

"Don't worry, just stand right here and don't say or do anything." With that I shoved my face right up near his and started shouting at him in German, preaching the love of God and the forgiveness of sin through the death of Jesus Christ. He stared at me and I continued, covering the *Four Spiritual Laws,* giving my testimony, and then starting all over.

I was shouting so loud at him that nearly a hundred kids crowded around to see what was going on. When I sensed their attention, I pulled away from Fred and began preaching to the crowd. I felt a special anointing of the Holy Spirit and I could sense His power working. I preached for several minutes as Fred and Fred worked their way through the crowd and passed out tracts. The Communists asked many questions and I was able to clearly show them the way to Christ. Then, of course, they too wanted autographs, so the three of us repeated the message on their scarves.

After about an hour of sharing with these kids, we were just bubbling over. There had been no hassles with the police, and everything had gone smoothly. Best of all, we had been shown that it didn't take lightning from the sky to open the ears and hearts of the Communists here at the Fest. God's leading was a very simple and direct approach to preaching to a crowd. We were overjoyed as we took a break for something to drink at a little restaurant.

Europeans are not a bit shy about sitting down at restaurant tables already occupied by strangers. So when we sat down and some kids heard us talking amongst ourselves in English, they immediately joined us and asked for our autographs on their scarves. This was going to be a *spiritual* feast! God led the people to us. They were all around us. All we had to do was start sharing.

The kids in the restaurant were even more receptive than the crowd outside had been. They seemed very interested and asked questions which led me to believe that some of them were not just trying to debate but were honestly searching. They had heard something appealing about a personal God whom they were taught didn't even exist. They wanted to hear more. I'm convinced that if we'd had more time with them in the restaurant that first evening, some of them would have received Christ. God knows.

When we left the restaurant, we almost got sucked into a bad situation. A group of kids had made a big circle, holding hands and skipping through the crowd. As they ran, they picked up more and more kids until they became a formidable bunch. They weaved in and out and around, picking up more and more people.

"What's this?" we asked.

"A game," they said. So we joined in, not realizing what was going on. We had been passing out tracts until they pulled us into their circle, and like dummies, we had gone along just to see what was going on. The game involved a girl running around the circle and grabbing a guy with her scarf. Then she would take him into the middle of the circle and plant a heavy kiss on him. Then he would take the scarf and run around the circle looking for another girl, and so on.

Fred Starkweather and I were together and we

agreed that this was no game for us, so we split. Fred Bishop was standing down the line from us and couldn't clearly see what the game was all about. So he was still involved without even knowing what he (a good married man) was involved in!

"Fred! Let's get out of here!" we called.

"No," he said, "this is fun!"

"Fred! Come on!" we shouted.

"Aw, take it easy," he whined. "I'm fixing to witness."

"Don't you see what they're doing?"

When we showed him, he realized this was no place to witness. We got out of there fast.

We learned a lesson from that. From that point on, we decided we would not try to witness from inside anyone else's circle. We would either form our own circle and witness from inside it, or we'd witness from the outside of the circles.

As we were leaving the festival around midnight I noticed three Russian sailors. I walked up to them and handed them a piece of paper, signifying that I wanted their autographs. As they signed, I said the only three words I knew in Russian: "Jesus loves you." They jumped back about two feet, gasping and dropping their pens. They didn't know what to think. I left them with Russian tracts, and we went on our way. Their reaction made me feel like a little boy who had cursed in the sanctuary of a conservative church.

The Russians were one of three groups which were the heroes of the Fest, as far as we could tell. It seemed that the delegates idolized first the Russians, then the North Vietnamese military men, and finally, the Communists from America. One of the reasons that *we* drew so many people so fast was that, until they heard what we had to say, many of the delegates thought we were American radicals.

I was surprised to learn that there were 600 American Communists at the World Fest. (If that isn't enough to make Christians get down on their knees and ask God to pour out His Spirit on our nation, then I don't know what will.)

I cannot describe the joy we felt that night on our way back to Wansee. All we could do on the train was sing and praise God. People thought we had flipped out, but we were just filled with the joy of the Lord. There were drunks lying around the Wansee station when we arrived. As we walked through, laughing and singing, they would rouse and slobber, "Wh'sh goin' on?"

We were like little kids. We had worried and wondered and prayed over how God would open the doors for us, and He had shown us that He was in charge. I felt a baptism of joy I had never known before. I had heard people talk about the holy giggles, and now I had a case of them myself. I just laughed and praised the Lord, and praised the Lord and laughed!

We stayed up until about two in the morning, sharing with Tex all that had gone on. I could hardly sleep, I was so keyed up. The time just wouldn't move fast enough for me. I had to get back over to Alexanderplatz.

Chapter Fifteen

DAY TWO: Revolutionaries

The most revolutionary people in the world ought to be the children of God. Wherever the devil has a stronghold, believers in Jesus Christ should be there sparking a spiritual revolution. Fred and Fred and I felt like revolutionaries in the midst of the Communist camp. When we arose the next morning, we knew we would have to spend much of the day in prayer in order to be prepared for the evening at the Fest.

I was trying to be careful lest I neglect Tex and Davey during those days. I spent some time with them at the lake in the morning, but I must admit that it was hard for me to concentrate on anything but the Fest. I wanted to be attentive to their needs, but I know I wasn't the husband and father I should have been right then. I was the victim of a real paradox. Here I was, in the middle of the most thrilling and important ministry in my life, on a super-spiritual high, yet I was incapable of giving proper attention to my family. I worried about it because I knew that any day could be my last on the free side of the border.

In prayer that day, Fred Starkweather felt led not to carry any literature across the border. Fred Bishop and I loaded ourselves down with tracts and stickers, and the three of us began the long, tedious process of being checked through the border. Praise God! The border guards pointed at one of us to be searched. Fred Starkweather.

They took him to the back room and he underwent an intensive frisking, but of course nothing was found. Truly, God was with us and would bless us again this day.

One of the rules of crossing the border was that you had to have the equivalent of five German marks converted into German currency, and you could not bring it back across the border with you. One great way to use our marks, we found, was to buy some of that delicious ice cream which had been flown in from Moscow just for the Fest. We discovered that if the Communists do one thing well, it is making ice cream.

As we walked around Alexanderplatz eating our ice cream that evening, it seemed that even more young people had gathered than on the previous night. The impact of their number didn't diminish. It still astonished us.

Things were a bit quieter in the plaza than they had been the night before. There didn't seem to be any natural openings for us to start witnessing. I began to feel impatient and uncomfortable. It was time to do something.

"Guys, listen," I said. "I think we need to get off somewhere and just pray."

"I don't think we need to get alone," Fred Bishop said. "I think we should kneel right here and pray."

Ten feet from us stood six Communist soldiers. "Hey," I said. "I don't think that would be too cool."

"Sam, I believe that's what God wants," Fred insisted.

"Maybe," I replied doubtfully, "but I just don't think so. We could go to prison."

"I thought we'd already settled that," Fred reminded me.

"Well, OK," I said. "If you really feel led, let's do it."

We knelt in a little cluster, right in the middle of Alexanderplatz with thousands of Communist young people milling about. Fred Starkweather prayed first. I could hear the people getting quieter. Then Fred Bishop prayed. I was shaking. I could hear feet shuffling closer to us. I felt the eyes of dozens of delegates and I was sure that they were staring at us in wonder. I kept my eyes closed tight.

Suddenly Fred was through praying. It was my turn. In Philippians 2:12, the Apostle Paul said to work out our salvation with fear and trembling. I was sure obeying that command! My voice was weak and shaky, and once I got started, I was afraid to quit. I had no idea what would greet us when we stopped. I continued with what had to be one of the longest public prayers in the history of my ministry.

Finally I came to the end of my prayer. It took all the holy boldness I could muster to say those last four words, "In Jesus name. Amen."

I knew a crowd had gathered, but I hardly noticed it as I rose. The Spirit of God came upon me with such fullness that I was *lifted* from my knees. Before I was fully erect, I began preaching the Gospel, and I continued preaching for four hours.

That in itself was a miracle, because I didn't know four hours' worth of German! Few times in my ministry had I felt the anointing of God so clearly as I spoke. He met my needs as I preached, quickening every word of German I had ever learned or heard. The crowd, which was originally about a hundred or so, grew as I preached. I didn't know where Fred and Fred had gotten to, but I kept preaching. I shared my testimony, the straight Gospel, the love of Christ, the need for confession and repentance from sin, the *Four Spiritual Laws,* and as much about the blood and power of the resurrected Christ as I could cram in. The Spirit made it all fit together and make sense, and it was obvious that God was at work in the hearts of the listeners as well.

Suddenly I noticed the Communist soldiers breaking through the crowd. I thought of Tex, of Davey, of Siberia, and of losing a decade or more of my precious freedom. I was worrying too much about what I had heard and read rather than trusting in the promise of God that His glory would be my rear guard. As the soldiers reached me I hesitated, waiting for those fateful words, "You're under arrest. We're taking you in."

They never came. Instead, they began firing me one question after another.

"Who is Jesus?"

"How do you know He's real?"

"How did Jesus come into your heart?"

It was incredible. The crowd picked up on the questions, asking the same things, everyone talking at once.

An atheist called for silence. "I don't believe in God," he said, "but this man has something to say and we must listen. The crowd is too large for those in the back to hear. Let's spread out and sit down!"

A young man quickly took off his coat and threw it beneath me. "You must not get dirty," he said, almost with reverence.

I sat and fielded questions, preaching to this multitude and being full of the joy of the Lord. There was no place in the world I would rather have been. Speaking to a half million people at an evangelistic crusade would not have compared to the unique opportunity I had there to share Christ with kids who had never heard and probably would never hear again. These were non-Christians, totally ignorant of the things of God. A love for them welled up within me and I felt an immense assurance that now, as never before, I was in the exact center of God's perfect will.

This was not merely something I did that God decided to bless. Nor was it something He *allowed* as part of His permissive will. No, this was a divinely planned event to which I had been called. I felt it was a preaching opportunity which would not come again in this century.

I don't generally put much stock in actions based on emotions, but I felt such a joy and such a love for these kids that I was simply bursting with the compassion of Christ. I loved them so much that I knew it had to be of God, for within me I didn't have the capacity for loving on such a scale. God was loving lost souls

through me. Though they were dedicated follow-
ers of a philosophy opposed to Christianity, God
loved them.

I saw that their hearts were hungry. Their
minds had been filled with the lies of Satan
from the time that they were born. I wanted to
give them all of Jesus that was in me.

After about four hours, I could hardly talk
any more. The words wouldn't come fast enough
to cover the thoughts I wanted to convey. One
boy asked me a question and I missed part of it.
I didn't understand the language well enough to
pick up everything.

As I turned my head to hear him better I
noticed a young girl with long brown hair, sitting in the crowd. A beautiful smile was on her
face and the Holy Spirit seemed to bear witness
immediately that she also was a child of God.
Could it be? I wondered. *Could this be one of
those underground believers I've heard so much
about?* She caught my eye and translated into
English the question I had not been able to understand. My heart flooded with joy as I became
convinced that she was a sister in Christ.

Finally I was exhausted. The crowd began to
break up a bit, and I stood to stretch. As I
moved to the edge of the crowd, young people
began to ask pointed questions. "How do I receive
Jesus?" "How do I pray?" "I want to believe; what
does it mean to believe?"

As I stood there talking with them the girl
with the long brown hair came by and said in
a confidential tone, "I cannot talk to you now.
If I am seen I will be in very much trouble.
There are people watching you who could mean
trouble for you. Can I meet you tomorrow?"

"Yes," I said. "At the fountain at 6:30."

After she disappeared into the crowd, I just stood there praising God. It looked as though I had made contact with an underground believer. The next evening we would meet at the huge fountain in the plaza and I would find out more about her and any other Christians at the Fest. She would probably know if there were others.

I went looking for Fred and Fred to tell them of the girl, but I couldn't find them. As I walked around the perimeter of Alexanderplatz, the fatigue and emotional drain hit me. I was spent. I saw the thousands and thousands of kids running in circles, singing and chanting and looking for causes, committed to revolution but not knowing the true Revolutionary. I knew what the Gospel writer meant when he said that Jesus saw the multitude and "felt compassion for them."

All I could do was weep. For an hour I walked around, almost in a daze, unable to contain the depth of my feeling for these young people. "How God? How can we reach them, just three of us and 100,000 of them?"

His words burned into my heart: "Trust Me. Trust Me. Trust Me."

"But Lord, surely there must be many churches in West Berlin and in all of West Germany. Where are the believers? Where are all the believers?"

God spoke to my heart: "Gideon's army was not a big army. It took only a few. And what I did with Gideon and his men, I will do with you if you will remain committed to Me and will trust Me."

I continued to walk and weep. All I could do was put my complete confidence in the Holy Spirit. I knew that our battle was spiritual and that the task ahead did not involve a battle with minds or bodies, but with the spirit. It was the Holy Spirit which gave me a broken heart for these people, a burden such as I had never before experienced. They were hungry, hungry, hungry. Hungry for the Bread of Life.

I felt fortunate that I had not been arrested, but I didn't know what might have happened to Fred and Fred. I could only pray and hope.

While threading my way through the crowd, I came upon a large group of people who seemed to be involved in debate. I thought I might get a chance to say something for Jesus, so I inched my way into the center, only to find Fred Bishop preaching the Gospel! In the middle of another little crowd nearby, Fred Starkweather was preaching.

What had happened, I learned later, was that the crowd had gotten so large when I was preaching that Fred and Fred went to the edges and started preaching too, employing Communists to interpret for them!

Fred Bishop was arguing with a black man about Communism and Christ. When he saw me in the circle, he asked me to take over. "I'm bushed," he said.

"Where is your Jesus?" the African communist demanded. "I can't see Him. I know what Communism is and what it is doing because I can see that, but I don't see Jesus."

The Lord gave me wisdom. I turned to a boy and girl who were holding hands. "Do you believe in love?" I asked.

"Yes," they snickered.

"Then where is it?" I asked. "Show it to me, I can't see it."

The black man got the point, then charged,

"I hear about all the love you Christians say you have, but you hate blacks."

I pointed my finger in his face and said, "Sir, eight years ago I would have hated you just because you are black. But now I can say to you in front of these people, quite honestly, that I love you in Jesus Christ." He was taken aback.

"Do you love people?" I went on.

"Yes," he said.

"Do you love Communists?"

"Yes, of course I do. I'm a socialist myself."

"Do you love capitalists?" I asked.

He stuttered, "Well, uh,—no."

"That's the point. Communists love Communists, and capitalists love capitalists, but only a believer in Jesus Christ can love every man. Only a person who knows God can even begin to understand love."

God had moved in a mighty way that night, not just in one group, but in three. We had all been preaching. The Lord had showed us that with just the three of us, He would build an army that would shake the Communist Youth World Fest for His Glory.

I thought the first night had been the happiest of my life, but the second night even topped that. After we got back and shared with Tex, I simply couldn't sleep. My mind's eye brought back the faces of countless hungry souls, and I prayed for each one as the sight played on my mind. It was a long time before I finally fell asleep, exhausted.

Chapter Sixteen

DAY THREE: Our First Souls

The next morning I spent some time with Tex and Davey down near the lake, but I confess I had a hard time keeping my mind on them. I felt bad, but there was little I could do. My mind was filled with what had happened the first two days at the Fest, and I wondered what would happen this day.

I wanted more than anything to give of myself to my family, but I was in the middle of such a heavy spiritual experience that I couldn't slow down enough. I could only pray that God would be their strength during these difficult days.

Late that afternoon Fred and Fred and I loaded ourselves with literature and prayed that none of us would be searched. We had the usual hassles waiting in line and getting our twenty-four-hour visas, but none of us were searched or even questioned. We ate in Alexanderplatz and then hurried to the fountain where we were to meet Ilse, the underground East German Christian girl who had introduced herself to me the day before. We were excited.

As we waited by the fountain, young people from all over the plaza approached us and asked if we were going to be talking about Jesus again. It thrilled me to know that they wanted to hear more. Many we recognized from the first two nights. We decided that God must have used the Communist women's magazine to stir up much interest in us. Rather than making the delegates antagonistic as the magazine people had hoped, the article had simply made them curious.

There were people everywhere looking for the *Jesus People*. We thought that the kids might be reacting a bit against their Communist leadership; for while the magazine instructed them on how to argue with us, it was rarely a *young* person who led the debates. *They* apparently wanted to defy the leadership and let us have our say. If this World Fest was supposed to be a world showcase exhibiting the freedom of speech allowed by the Communists, then the young people were going to see that it happened.

Some of the young people pointed out other Communist kids who were lying in the grass, lounging, talking and playing. "Do you know why they're doing that?" they would ask us.

"No, why?" (It didn't appear so unusual to us.)

"Because when the Fest is over and they return to their own countries, they will not be allowed such leisure time again. The only reason they are not being hassled now is because all the news media from all over the world are watching."

More and more kids came up to see if we would be preaching that night. "Yes," I said. "We'll be talking about Jesus in about half an hour. Right now we're waiting for someone."

Finally Ilse showed up. She brought her brother and her girl friend also. We spent about five minutes getting acquainted and introducing each other all around; then we asked how they had become Christians, where they worshipped, etc. Hearing the name of Jesus in just normal conversation brought the Communist kids from all over. "They're talking about Jesus again," they said. "They're going to start preaching soon."

It was amazing to us to see how God used something different each day, and each day it was something less unusual. The first day we had written the plan of salvation on their autograph scarves, and the second day we had knelt to pray in their midst. Now we had an audience of a hundred or so, just by mentioning the name of Jesus in normal conversation.

I began to preach and more young people swarmed around. Fred and Fred moved to the edge of the crowd and began preaching, breaking off clusters of Communists to keep the groups small. But somehow the whole gathering seemed to have heard about us and had been watching and waiting for us. All three of us had crowds too big to handle.

What a thrill it was for me to see Ilse, her brother, and her girl friend split up and take on groups of their own! They shared their testimonies, explaining to any who would listen what God had done in their lives. I learned later that it was a real step of faith for Ilse, as she had been warned almost a year earlier by the police that she should never again talk about Christ in public. She hadn't done so in eleven months, but now she was joyous for the chance.

God had moved in a strange and wonderful way, increasing our witness from one preacher the first night, to three the next night, and now to six. We had a half dozen groups of Communists gathered around and listening intently to this "new idea": a God who lives and loves.

This was the night the Communist leadership began to take us seriously. Our number had doubled overnight, and they were no longer content to simply ignore us, assuming that the young people would do likewise. It was obvious that the delegates *were* listening and were in fact waiting for us and watching for us and talking about us. And the young people had lots of questions and wanted answers to some very direct inquiries.

When the opposition really started, it came from the adults. They asked all the "right questions" and voiced all the canned objections of the Organization. They had learned their parts well— so well that they all sounded like broken records. I'm sure the Communist young people noticed the same thing, and in a way, it made them want to take our side. We were nonconformists, and we appealed to them somehow.

The adults wouldn't have us arrested because they knew this would cause an international scene; after all, the world press was there. So they not only permitted the communist kids to lounge in the grass, but they let us speak our piece. Arresting us would only make it appear that they took us seriously and considered us a threat. They didn't want to admit that to anyone.

I was really beginning to feel my oats, and as often happens in such a situation, I slipped into a fleshly argument. We had acknowledged that we would be able to do nothing outside of God's power, and there was no doubt that He was the One who had opened these doors to preach and witness. But as we got excited about the opportunities, I somehow allowed myself the thought that we had in some way been responsible for pulling something off.

A Communist from Israel shouted me down while I was preaching, claiming that he had spent time in Chicago and knew that Christians were rip-off artists who took money from the poor and gave it to the capitalists. Since I had lived in Chicago, I knew I would be able to tell if he were saying anything accurately or not. He said, "I worked for a long time with *Chinese For Christ* and I know they just took people's contributions and didn't use them for the ministry!"

Suddenly I was angry. I said, "You listen here! I lived in Chicago and I know that organization! They're solid and they're honest! What you're saying is just not true!"

I was speaking in the flesh, and though I knew I was right, it was wrong to deal with him on his own level.

"You calling me a liar?" he demanded, grabbing me by the shirt and pulling me to face him. I was infuriated.

"Yes, I am!" I shouted. But in that instant, I fell under conviction. The Spirit of God spoke to my heart, showing me that I would never win an argument by shouting and debating. I could only conquer the situation for Jesus by letting God love the man through me. I felt bad and immediately apologized.

"I'm sorry I yelled at you," I said.

"You calling me a liar?" he demanded again.

"All I want to say to you is that Jesus loves you."

"I'll tell you something about your Jesus," he sneered, doubling his fist and waving it in my face. "Are you still going to say Jesus loves me when I smash this fist in your face and fill your mouth with blood?"

The Lord gave me instant wisdom and an answer, though I was scared. "Man, if you hit me, I just pray that every drop of blood that comes from my mouth will remind you of the blood of Jesus that was shed for you."

"I ought to kill you!" he said, rearing back to slug me. The crowd jumped away from us.

"Jesus loves you," I said again.

"You *want* me to hit you?" he asked, incredulous.

"Go ahead, hit me right now. I'm willing to put my life on the line for Jesus Christ. Go ahead."

He turned and stomped off. I shivered. Two Free German Youth approached me. "We've never seen so much love in our lives," one said. "How can *we* have that kind of love?"

"Praise God, Jesus Christ can give it to you if you'll give yourselves to Him. If you want Jesus in your heart, you can pray and ask Him."

To my surprise, they said, "We would like to do that."

Praise God! He had used a bad situation to glorify Himself. I knew the Communists could win all the arguments they wanted, but they had no defense against our loving them through the Spirit.

"Would you like to pray and receive Jesus right now?" I asked.

"No," they said. "Not with everyone watching."

"Then when you get home tonight and you are alone, pray and ask Jesus to come into your heart and forgive your sins."

They said they would, and promised to tell me about it the next day. They had heard the plan of salvation preached, and now they had seen Christianity in action. The Christ of the cross had drawn them to Himself. And to think that I had almost blown it by reacting initially in the flesh.

A couple of university girls came up and asked if they could talk with me alone. "We want what you have been talking about," they said.

We walked away from the crowds and sat on some steps near Alexanderplatz. As I told them that Jesus loved them and wanted them for His own, it was obvious that the Spirit had been working in their hearts.

"We want to know Jesus," they said. "But it costs so much here. When we were in eighth grade we had to make a choice. We could either join the Communist party and become Free German Youth, or we could join the church. If you join the church you cannot complete your education, and you cannot get a good job. At that age, it was too big a decision to make. We, along with ninety-five per cent of the other people our age, chose to join the Free German Youth. But now we feel terrible about it."

"Listen," I said, "God knows and understands your hearts. God will forgive and cleanse you and will set you free. He can give you a new life in spite of your circumstances and surroundings. But you must be willing to start with Him now."

"But you don't know what it will cost," one of

119

them said. "At the university a girl stated publicly that she had given her life to Christ, and they kicked her out. And she had had good grades. This girl was a friend of mine."

"Jesus Christ gave His all for you," I said. "Are you willing to give your all for Him?" That was a painful thing for me to say to those young girls. I could never really know what it was going to cost them, yet I knew that if I asked *them* to pay the price, God would expect me to be willing to do the same. In my heart, because of Jesus, I was ready to do that. And so were the girls.

"Yes," they said. "We are willing." We bowed our heads and prayed right there, and I knew that I was praying with converts who had more at stake because of their decisions than anyone I had ever prayed with before.

When I finally turned my attention to what was happening with the others at Alexanderplatz, I noticed that the crowds were still surrounding Fred and Fred, Ilse, her brother, and girl friend. The discussions were still going hot and heavy, but it was obvious that God had taught them the same lesson He had taught me. Though the adult Communists were arguing and getting mad, the Christians were just loving them through it.

It was a tremendous blessing to my heart to see Ilse, her friend, and brother putting their freedom on the line for Jesus. There was always the chance that we Americans would be prosecuted, but more than likely we would simply be thrown out and banned from the Fest and maybe the country. But these German kids faced certain imprisonment if they were arrested.

When things broke up Tuesday night, our new friends from East Germany invited us to go with them to Church the next evening. The leaders of the Fest had decided to permit one church service for each night, as long as it was orderly and held inside the church building. It sounded interesting to us, so we agreed to meet them in Alexanderplatz at 5:30 the next evening.

When we got back to Wansee, Tex was overjoyed to hear of our first converts, and we were excited because Jeff, his brother Jim, and Skip moved into the cabin with us for the rest of the Fest. They would be joining us in the ministry for the remainder of the activities, and this would be a great addition because of Jeff's ability to speak German and Russian fluently. Of course, the increased manpower would multiply our efforts too.

Chapter Seventeen

DAY FOUR: A March *Here*?

Tex, Davey, and I had been invited to supper at the home of our old friends in West Germany, the Haases. It turned out to be just the thing our family needed. I arranged to meet Fred and Fred near the border, along with Jeff, Jim, and Skip. We then took a bus with Tex and Davey to visit the Haase home.

On the way, Satan made another attempt to stop our witnessing by attacking Tex. She began to make it clear to me that she didn't appreciate the fact that I was neglecting Davey. She said he was becoming irritable because he didn't have his daddy with him as much as he needed to. That bothered Tex, of course, and made her irritable, too.

It hurt me that Satan had attacked us this way. He went right at the core of my being, my happy family. Nothing else could have hindered me at such a time, but Satan knew if he could shake things up in my home, he would throw a monkey wrench into the works.

Tex has been just the perfect wife for me, and I have always been aware of all the hardships she must endure following a country preacher-boy all over the world, sometimes not knowing if I would return. Many times we didn't know where our next meal would come from.

It was natural that Tex should fall prey to temptation more easily than the rest of us. While we were out where the action was, she washed our clothes and had meals waiting for us when we got back late each night. She kept us going with all the practical things so necessary to our ministry. Hers was not a ministry in the limelight as ours was. We were on the frontlines of the battle, seeing God work. She always got the news second hand, and I'm sure it made her feel less than an equal in the action.

Yet I knew that she was as important as any of us. She was indispensable. While her ministry was a humble and selfless one with little obvious rewards, it was one she continued to work at diligently. It was hard for her with me gone every evening and most of every night.

With as much love as I had within me, I looked her in the eye and said, "Baby, I love you. But please, you're going to have to bear with me for awhile longer. This is the most important and greatest opportunity for witness we will probably ever have together."

Tex admitted that most of her problem was the constant worry over my safety. It was hard to wait up every night, not knowing what might have happened. Then right in the middle of her almost-unbearable tension, we would burst in with our stories of how wonderful everything had been

—not remembering that she had been home just worrying and praying and waiting. I know how insensitive I must have seemed.

Praise the Lord that Herr Haase was sensitive to the Holy Spirit. He asked Tex if she and Davey would like to go on a boat ride with him and his wife and their cousin. It was just the thing for Tex, because while the Haases didn't speak much English at all, their cousin did. She would have something to do and someone to talk to while I was gone. A peaceful trip on the Wansee River would soothe her.

Meanwhile I left after supper to meet the other four guys at the central train station in West Berlin. As we walked toward the train which would take us across the border, I was finally hit with the immense pressure which had been building up within me. Hadn't we been through enough already? It was taking me longer to get to sleep every night. I was tired.

Depression hit hard. I wanted to give in to Tex and spend an evening with her and Davey. All I could see ahead was another night of Communist leaders screaming and yelling in my face. I nearly stumbled as my physical strength suddenly drained away. Slumping forward, I said, "Guys, I can't make it. I just can't make it. If I go tonight it will take a miracle of God to bring me through."

They were shocked at my reaction to the tension. I had been the leader. This whole mission had originated from God's direction to me. And here I was, the first one to break. It was at this point that Fred and Fred received special understanding about why they were here. I needed them. Without them I could never have stood up to the onslaught of the evil one.

The guys gathered around me and took me to a corner where they prayed for me and laid hands on me. The Lord refreshed me with His peace and strength, and we were able to go on.

I'll admit, though, that I was still simply going in obedience rather than in the fullness of joy and enthusiasm I had had during the first three days. But I was about to get a "shot in the arm."

As we crossed the border, Jeff and Fred Bishop were chosen to be searched and questioned. They were the only two of the six of us who had been led to carry nothing across! All Jeff had was his guitar. They checked it carefully, and of course, found nothing. I knew God would be our strength again.

Our East German Christian friends gave us a lesson in physical fitness as we walked a brisk mile with them from the fountain in Alexanderplatz to the church. When we arrived, a bunch of young people had gathered outside and a young man was playing a guitar and singing praises to Jesus. We said, "Praise the Lord, this is our kind of people," and joined in the singing.

One of the church fathers, very dignified, emerged from the church to break up the impromptu session. "You know the Party has allowed you one hour each night only if you will confine yourselves to the church building," he stated firmly. The young people agreed and went inside submissively.

It was obvious to all six of us that the Party had allowed this "freedom" of worship in order to confine the Christians to the church building and to keep them from having any influence on the Fest. Also, they could keep an eye on the kids and know who was who so they could report all activities to the Party.

The service was an hour long and was read by a boring speaker who all but put us to sleep. It was gross. There was nothing there for these lively young Christians. As soon as it was over, the young people again congregated outside and struck up with their guitars and songs. All six of us stayed to see what would happen. About a hundred other young people joined in this time, and it was great.

The church father came out again and reminded the young people that such activity was not permitted outside the church. We half expected the kids to submit again. Instead, one of the kids said, "OK, we'll leave. Let's march to Alexanderplatz for Jesus!"

I could hardly believe it. I have been involved in a lot of Jesus walks and marches in my day, but this would be something else. A Jesus march in the middle of the Communist Youth World Fest!

Jeff joined the front of the group with his guitar (there were about six others with guitars), and we started out, singing for Jesus and marching a hundred strong down the middle of the street.

About halfway to Alexanderplatz, we were met by an official from the church and an official of the government. "You cannot do this," they said. "It is an act of provocation and will be considered a criminal offense. You must decide. Are you going to confine your activity to the church, or are you going to commit this criminal offense?"

A young man from the back of the crowd shouted, "We have already decided! We are following Christ! Let's go to Alexanderplatz!"

Another said, "The Free German Youth claim

126

that there's freedom at Alexanderplatz! Let's exercise this freedom for Jesus Christ!"

I was amazed. We had not instigated it. These kids were on their own, yet they displayed a holy boldness. The Spirit had instigated it. I was thrilled.

When they got to Alexanderplatz, however, some of the kids became fearful. The sight of Party members eyeing them and writing names in their report books absolutely freaked them out. Just then, one of their leaders suggested, "Let's sing our songs in Hebrew or Latin so no one will understand."

Well, of course, this kept the authorities away, but it also spoiled the witness because none of the other delegates could understand the words either. So the crowd which had gathered in the plaza to see what the Jesus People were up to fizzled out and broke up because the singing didn't communicate.

As the Christians broke up and moved away, about fifteen of them came to me. "Sammy," they said, "we want to go all the way for Jesus. Will you lead us so we can make an impression on Alexanderplatz for Jesus Christ?"

"OK," I said. "Follow me." With the six of us and fifteen of them, we made a good sized little band, playing and singing songs of praise to God. The Communists thought it was some kind of game, so they joined in. As we circled Alexanderplatz, we kept picking up more and more marchers, only a few of whom were Christians. By the time we had circled the place once we were about a hundred strong, and the Communist onlookers didn't know what to make of it. Their favorite argument had been, "Why should we trust Jesus? There's 100,000 of us and just a few of you!"

That logic was gone now! We had been just three the first day—then six—then more than twenty; now it appeared that we had won at least a hundred delegates! Three or four guitars were going and we were singing. The Communists were getting panicky, thinking we had finally revived the whole place. Then Jeff and I were led to give our testimonies. The Spirit was really moving.

While I was speaking, one of the adult antagonists tried to get into the act. "You have simply been propagandized there in America," he shouted. "It's just a lie of the capitalists!"

Before I could say anything, one of the underground Christians stood. "I'm from East Germany," he said, "and I want to tell you that Jesus Christ is in my heart and is real to me."

I preached some more and it was obvious that the Communists were really beginning to see us in a new light. We were a threat. We were making inroads. Jeff shared his testimony and a Communist agitator jumped up and started screaming at him. I turned to him and said, "Sir, Jesus Christ came into my life and changed me."

He turned on me—which is what I wanted. If I could take the heat off Jeff, he could continue with his testimony. I backed away as the man came toward me, shouting and arguing. We got off to the side and I sat with him on the grass. Fred and Fred saw what was happening and went to their knees in intercession for me. The Spirit of God moved in the man's life, and by the time we were finished talking, not only had he been kept from disrupting Jeff's effective ministry, but he had also been touched by God.

He had tears in his eyes as he said, "I'm really thankful that I came here and talked to you tonight. You've given me so much to think about." I had simply shared with him that we were sincere and that we had not been victimized by propaganda. We had experienced for ourselves the power of the resurrected Christ in our lives.

Later, as I preached, a man challenged me to show him what Jesus Christ had done for the people in the two thousand years since His birth. He said he could see that Communism had put food in starving stomachs, but he couldn't see anything Jesus had done for people. Just then I noticed some crippled Korean girls who were being pushed around Alexanderplatz in wheelchairs, so I challenged him to bring them to me.

"I will get my Christian brothers here and we will pray that God will heal them and raise them out of those chairs." I was honestly disappointed when he backed away in fear and would not accept the challenge. I don't go in for sensationalism, and I have only rarely seen dramatic healings in my ministry, but I am as convinced now as I was then that God would have honored our prayer for His glory that night.

I ran into the two young men who had promised the night before that they would receive Christ when they got home alone.

"Did you get alone and pray?" I asked.

"Yes, we did," they said, beaming.

"What happened?"

"Praise God," they said. "Jesus is in our hearts."

They were just thrilled with their new Savior, and I could only praise Jesus.

The officials were getting uptight as more and more young people came to the point where they wanted to pray and receive Christ. Delegates were approaching any of us that they recognized as Jesus People (though we had never called ourselves that) and asking if we would lead them to Christ.

Finally, official word came to us. A man came to Fred and me and said distinctly, "If you do not stop this, you will all be arrested."

The time had come for a decision. Should we stop? Or should we risk imprisonment? By this time I was so full of God that I had no fear for myself. But what about the twenty or so new believers? They might not be so sure. I didn't want to take them all to prison with me, so I said, "Listen, we're going to have to break up and quit or we'll all wind up in prison."

A girl looked at me with sad determination in her eyes. "Sammy," she said, "we have met Jesus Christ. He has changed our lives. You have told us that He gave His all for us, and now we are willing to give our all for Him. If you want to quit now, you can cross the border and go back to West Berlin. We can't do that, and we don't want to. We are going to continue to share Jesus Christ."

All I could do was pray, "God forgive me."

After quickly mapping out a new strategy, we told them to just walk around and we would get back together with them soon. Then the six of us walked through Alexanderplatz, pretending to leave the young people. We were followed all the way to the edge of the crowd by plainclothesmen. They stood not more than a hundred feet from us and waited as we prayed for guidance.

By this time, we had gotten pretty good at losing people in crowds and on trains, especially after our experience with Checkpoint Charlie. We decided that we would head for the train station, but that I would get lost in the crowd and make my way back to the believers. I would then take them to a somewhat secluded park we had noticed near the church. We would meet there for a discipling meeting. I was beginning to get convicted by the fact that we'd won some new Christians, but hadn't thought about helping them grow. God's command was to go and make disciples, not just to evangelize.

I made it back to the believers all right and took them to the park. For a half hour before Fred and Fred, Jeff, Jim, and Skip got there, I just taught them new truth from the Word. They drank it in. When the others arrived, we had a good old-fashioned prayer meeting.

We could be seen vaguely from the road and a few other young people came out of curiosity. Two received Christ that night, and we rejoiced over souls being won even during a time of discipleship. We knew the Spirit was doing a fantastic work.

I can't describe the feeling of love I developed for those kids. Their boldness, their openness, their hunger for the Word just endeared them to me. These were twentieth century young people living in the dark ages of oppression—yet they had decided for Jesus through the simple preaching of the Gospel. They had counted the cost. It was no trip, no joy ride. It wasn't something they had done because someone else had. It wasn't something they had done because of parental pressure or the emotional appeal of an evangelistic service. These kids had made the most unpopular and difficult decision anyone in the world could make. No wonder I wanted them to have all there was of Jesus.

I knew that much of the success we had had was due to the faithfulness of the believers in the States who had promised to pray for us. Many times during our preaching and witnessing we could feel the presence of the Spirit protecting us. It was almost as if we could hear the covering prayers of our spiritual body at home, and it helped us go on.

This became the most beautiful day of my life. I recalled how Satan had attacked so forcefully, making me think I was too weak to cross the border that day. But he could not prevail against the cross of Christ.

Tex was happy to hear about all that had happened. She also had been renewed by a wonderful evening with the Haases. God gave her the strength to carry on and to understand. This was a day I would remember always. I was humbled that God had chosen to make me part of it.

Chapter Eighteen

DAY FIVE: Meeting in Secret

We learned from some of the Christian young people from the Free German Youth that the Party leaders had taught sessions each morning on how to combat our ministry. Each night the session leaders would watch to see what tactics we were using, and would then plan how to mess us up; then they would explain their strategy to the young people the next morning.

What they didn't realize was that it was the Holy Spirit who was giving us the tactics, and He never gave us the same idea twice. We didn't know what we were going to do until we did it, so whatever they thought they were prepared for was always a disappointment for them. Anyway, even if they did know what the Spirit had planned, how does one go about defeating the ideas of God? Impossible!

We didn't know what to expect Thursday night.

We knew they would be out for us after the warning we had received from the police. And with the Free German Youth being trained to stifle us, we knew they would be psyched up after the way we had triumphed the night before. We were leery and a bit frightened, but we had so much to thank God for and so many victories to remember that we were able to trust Him.

In prayer before crossing the border, I considered the idea of concentrating on discipleship training, rather than trying to win more souls at the Fest. The Lord immediately convicted my heart and I saw that this was a cop-out. He had led us here for evangelism and discipleship. It would have been the natural thing to evangelize until the heat came on and then sneak off for discipleship, but God was having no part of that.

The easiest part of our day on Thursday was getting across the border. From there on, it was cloak-and-dagger and hassle all the way. Our first appointment was an underground meeting at the home of a believer. This group would then take us to meet with yet another underground group, the latter made up mostly of Catholic Christians.

At the first meeting, I saw what Communism had done for its people. I had lived on North Kenmore Avenue in Chicago for two years, so I knew what slums look like. But this was worse than any slums I had seen. And this was supposed to be an average neighborhood.

The brother in charge of the meeting was really excited about Jesus. He introduced us to two Catholic theology students from a Czechoslovakian seminary. They were born-again believers, and I'll tell you, those priests loved Jesus! We had immediate rapport and fellowship as brothers in Christ and it was a beautiful worship experience.

Then we went on to a little clearing in the woods where we met underground Christians from Hungary, Poland, both sides of Germany, and of course, Czechoslovakia. Each shared something different about how the Party treated Christians in his particular country. It seems that each place differed in the degree of security and pressure applied by the Communists. Czechoslovakia is the worst place, with Hungary and East Germany next. Russia is bad too, of course, but there is an interesting difference between Russia and East Germany.

In Russia, Christians are forbidden to meet as Christians and hold baptisms and the like unless they have government permission. In East Germany and Czechoslovakia it is illegal to meet for any reason with people from the West.

As we stood there in that wooded sanctuary, we realized that our East German hosts could have been imprisoned because of our very presence. We cherished the time. We imagined that this must be the way the first century Christians met during the height of their persecution. What beautiful fellowship we had together, not as Catholic and Protestant, but as brothers and sisters in Christ!

We learned that when the chips are down and your life is on the line, you either hold a ceremonious ritual and turn your back on the real Truth, or you get right with Jesus. I had seen many Christians on the free side of the curtain who couldn't stand a little peer pressure; but behind the iron curtain are Christians who live for Christ at the daily risk of prison.

After someone shared from each country, we

were asked to minister. For a couple of hours we shared testimonies and songs, and I preached. Our little church there in the woods was the most precious meeting place I have ever been in. There were many new believers, and we just had a blessed time.

By the time we got to Alexanderplatz, the new believers were eagerly awaiting us. The Communists were wondering where we had been too, eager to head us off with some newly-learned strategy. We banded together, formed a circle, and started singing our Christian songs. Immediately the Communist young people surrounded us. The crowds were bigger than ever because we were the talk of the Fest by now.

I began to preach, but this time the adult Communists didn't try to challenge me. They just sent the young people in to surround us and sing loud songs. We tried to sing our own choruses louder, but we were no match for the 300 or so Communists. We were not sure what to do until the Spirit impressed upon me to begin singing *We Shall Overcome*.

This song had originally been a Christian song, but was then used by peace groups and racial groups, and we had heard it often at the Fest. It had become the young Communists' theme song. When we broke into that number they looked delighted—certain they had caught us off guard. Thinking we were singing their song, they joined right in.

All of us, believers and Communists, were singing a rousing version of *We Shall Overcome*—that is, until the Communists ran out of verses about peace and unity. Then we were ready and caught *them* off guard. We sang our Christian words, *We shall be like Him*, and *Jesus Christ loves*

136

you—and the Communists were freaked out. They had been sucked into singing *our* song! They ran to their leaders to see what to do next, making room for more interested Fest delegates who wanted to hear what we were preaching about. We had freedom to preach uninterrupted for the rest of the night.

The Spirit was touching more hearts and bringing more communists to Jesus. A thrilling thing for me was to hear brand new believers making up their own words to our little choruses. We would sing *God is so good,* and then change the words to *God answers prayer*; then a new believer would sing, *He's coming soon, He's coming soon, He's coming soon. He's so good to me.*

By now there were nearly a hundred of us with more coming to Christ hourly and putting their freedom on the line. I taught them a Jesus cheer ("Give me a J, give me an E," etc., in their own language). In America, Jesus cheers have become meaningless fads in many cases, but when underground Christians shout for their Lord, it's like heavenly music. After we'd spell out the name, I'd ask, "What's His name?" and they'd shout "JESUS!" at the top of their lungs. They repeated the response each time I'd ask, "Who is God's Son?" or "Who does the world need?" Everyone should see kids cheer for Jesus like that.

Fred and Fred were giving out some of our Jesus stickers, and they became like gold. Everyone wanted some to stick and some to give away, but they also wanted to keep some too, because Jesus stickers were something entirely new.

We praised God all the way back to Wansee that night. I noticed something strange when we crossed the border, though. While the East Germans had been attracted to us, people on the West side ran from us. How sad that people who can worship God in freedom take that freedom for granted! That may be the reason why there seems to be a church on every corner in America, and few believers out sharing their faith with the hungry people of the world.

But we had a right to praise God, didn't we? We had a new family of some 100 Christians who loved us for what we shared with them, and whom we loved for their dedication, enthusiasm, and boldness.

Chapter Nineteen

DAY SIX: Showers of . . .

By Friday we were exhausted and had to lean on the Lord for every physical step. The Fest had been a consistent and terrible drain on our systems, and we had just about had it.

Our plan that evening was to meet some of the believers at a little Lutheran church and spend much of the evening in discipleship. When we arrived, the small room was packed out.

Among the hundred or so young people was a little old lady of probably eighty years. After I had spent over an hour teaching about the Spirit-filled life and growth in Christ, she approached. She gave me a small notebook holder and a wall plaque which was inscribed in German, *We are truly brothers in Christ*. She was the only elderly person there, and her gift touched me. Inside the notebook she had written, "Blessed are you when men revile you and persecute you for My name's sake." It was a token of love and appreciation for our ministry there, and I still cherish it.

After spending a little more time rooting and grounding the new believers in the Word, I could see they were anxious to get back to Alexanderplatz. I tried to talk them out of it. "Why don't we spend the rest of the evening in discipleship?" I suggested.

"Oh, no," they said. "This is the chance of a lifetime. We may never again get the chance to be missionaries. This is our chance to evangelize the whole world by reaching the kids from all the different nations at Alexanderplatz." I understood and agreed.

We headed back toward the Fest 100 strong, and I mean *strong*. On the way, one underground believer told me he would rather be a Christian in a Communist country than in a free country.

"Why?" I asked.

"Because we are like trees," he explained. "The oppression is a great weight which pushes down on our top branches, and it makes our trunk and roots strong. In a free country we wouldn't have the pressure and our roots would not become as strong." It was a heavy truth, and an indictment for me as a Christian in a free country.

When we got to Alexanderplatz, the Communists were waiting for us. They immediately surrounded us with more than 500 young people who boomed out the chant, "Peace! Friendship! Solidarity against the imperialists!" They chanted louder and louder until their entire throng was screaming as if at a soccer game. There was no way we could sing, cheer, testify, or preach. All we could do was stand there helplessly while the uproar grew louder.

"Peace!"

"Friendship!"

"Solidarity against the imperialists!"

We could think of no counterattack, and yet we didn't want to run away. We joined hands and fell to our knees. "God, what would You have us do?" we prayed. He indicated that we do nothing. We would not have to battle this mighty force ourselves. The Communists didn't know Whom they were up against. Blessed be the name of the Lord, they thought they were coming against man, against some backwoods evangelists from America who had stolen away some of their number.

But, no, they were coming against God Almighty Himself. As we prayed, seeking His will, we wondered what would stop the chanting, what could drown out such hateful, boisterous noise. In an instant we knew. Lightning flashed and thunder rolled and torrents of rains whooshed onto Alexanderplatz. There was no fading out. The cheering and chanting stopped abruptly and the 500 young people who had been commissioned to frustrate us were running in every direction to escape the showers meant just for them.

Keeping our hands joined, we Christians moved quickly under a protective awning which had room in it for a couple of thousand people. It quickly filled with delegates from all over the plaza, and suddenly we had a captive audience. As the rain continued, the delegates had nothing to do but listen. We didn't want them to be bored just because the rain had temporarily halted the fun at the Fest. We proclaimed the Gospel to them freely the rest of the night, our detractors having split for other cover. I must have preached five different times that night as we all shared, witnessed and testified to the love of Jesus. We doubled our number that night as we saw the total of believers jump to around 200.

I understood in a new way the part of John 1:12 which says that God grants people the power to become the sons of God, "even to them that *believe* on his name." That had always puzzled me, but now I knew what it meant. Just the act of saying "I believe in Jesus" brought instant conversion. In a free country that would not be the case, for most people would freely say, "I believe in Jesus," though it means nothing to them. But when Communist delegates from all over the world heard the Gospel preached in East Germany and then made the statement, "I believe in Jesus," they were actually saying, "I'm willing to take a stand for something which may cost me my freedom, my family—even my life—because I believe that Jesus is Lord." When these people "believe on His name," brother, they are saved!

That night remains a highlight in my ministry. I never dreamed when God sent me to the Communist Youth World Fest that He would let me see 200 young people give their hearts to Him, especially under such circumstances. This was a convicting time for me which would come to mind many times in the future when I felt that God was leading me to do something which was too difficult or uncomfortable. If these young people, in the primes of their lives, can risk everything for God, I can certainly trust Him fully.

We had moved into the realm of the authority of the resurrected Christ. Satan might be able to come against *us*, but he cannot come against the body of Jesus Christ, for it is written that the gates of hell shall not prevail against it. Hallelujah! Glory to God! Praise the Lord Jesus Christ! God was so good.

Chapter Twenty

DAY SEVEN: Trouble

The Fest would officially end on Sunday at around noon, so our last evening for witnessing at the plaza was Saturday. I'm glad the Lord didn't show me the frightening things we would encounter, because I probably wouldn't have gone. I received first-hand experience in the kind of persecution I was bringing upon these young people by sharing Christ with them. It wasn't pretty, but of course, God was glorified in the triumphant end.

We had spent some time together at the home of an underground believer (who could be prosecuted just for entertaining foreigners), sharing the Word and eating supper together. By this time the believers had waxed bold and they sang choruses loudly even with the windows open.

As we were preparing to leave for Alexanderplatz, we were met at the door by the police who demanded to see all of our passports. I knew we were in trouble then; while most of the people there were East German young people registered for the Fest, a Czechoslovakian and I were foreigners and could be responsible for the imprisonment of the believer who owned the house.

I handed my passport to the officer, fully expecting to be arrested and to see our host arrested as well. I prayed that the Lord would miraculously intercede. He did! The officer opened my passport, ignoring it as he slipped my twenty-four-hour visa from it. He studied it for a moment, but of course my nationality was listed only in my passport and not in my visa.

"All right," he said, handing it to me. I breached a sigh of relief and a prayer of thanks.

The Czechoslovakian didn't have his passport! Our hearts skipped a beat as they demanded, "Where is yours?" He ran upstairs and found it, and they looked only at his visa as well. God was with us.

At Alexanderplatz, I met a young man who had read about our ministry in a book called *The Jesus Generation Also in Europe.* The book had been smuggled to him in East Germany, and he had come looking for me. Our being there was a blessing to him, and he began to spread the word throughout occupied European countries that we had come to the World Fest to share Jesus. It was an encouragement to the underground believers who had been suffering persecution for their faith.

The Free German Youth were determined to stop us on this final night. They had been frustrated in every attempt during the week, and they came "loaded for bear." There were more than a thousand of them to surround our small band of 200, and when they began their incessant cheering again, we just dropped to our knees again. Right on cue, God sent the rain again.

But this time the Free German Youth were ready for us. As we joined hands and moved under cover, they didn't split and run in all directions. Rather, they stayed right with us. They regrouped and when we started to preach, they started in again with, "Peace! Friendship! Solidarity!" We could not be heard. They had signs and slogans and were dominating the situation. I prayed.

God spoke to me. "Have a Jesus march," He said.

"Let's march for Jesus!" I shouted, and the 200 Christians rose as one and began to move out from under cover and into the rain. The Free German Youth weren't going to let us get far. They fell right in behind us and kept their chanting going, following us all around Alexanderplatz as we led the way, singing and praising God. To the thousands and thousands of other delegates, it looked as if there were twelve hundred Christians marching for Jesus!

Their minds were blown. People began running everywhere, asking each other, "What are we going to do? The Jesus People are coming!" We kept changing direction, stopping briefly to give a Jesus cheer, and then continuing. All over Alexanderplatz, panicking Communists came running to see how we had grown to such proportions. By now there were close to two thousand Communists following us and shouting as we continued to march and praise the Lord. After stopping for a quick Jesus cheer, we saw we were trapped in a corner of the plaza. We tried to keep going, but the two thousand Communists locked arms and surrounded us, shouting their slogans and holding us in!

As they jeered and shouted and screamed at us, thousands upon thousands of delegates from all over Alexanderplatz came running to see what was going on. We found ourselves in the middle of a sea of shouting Communists, and many people on the edges of the crowd wondered what in the world was going on.

An old German man tried to shout for silence. A few fell silent to see what he had to say. "We are all for peace, friendship, and solidarity," he said. "But that comes only through Jesus Christ!" Immediately he was drowned out by the snarling Communists who were now shaking their fists at us. I looked at one of the guys who had been leading our march. He was signaling to me (with his palms pressed together under his chin) that we should pray. I nodded and we knelt, 200 believers following our lead.

It was an incredible scene. I felt very vulnerable there on my knees, surrounded by 2,000 antagonists and thousands more spectators. As I prayed, God spoke clearly to my heart: "You'll never again get the chance to preach to this many lost people in your life. This may be the greatest opportunity you'll ever have to tell Communists about Me. Stand up and preach about Jesus."

"Lord," I cried, "Your strength and Your power will have to be with me. I can't do it on my own."

After calling for silence, and surprisingly getting it (they thought I, as the leader, was about to confess, apologize, or something), I went into a rapid-fire tirade about how Jesus could change a person's life and how He had changed mine.

146

The Lord quickened me to preach as fast as I could. I said more words in a few minutes than I ever thought possible.

The two thousand Free German Youth burst forward, nearly trampling the 200 Christians and pushing in toward me, swinging their fists in my face and threatening me. The whole place was in an uproar as the crowd surged forward. For a second, I honestly thought I had preached my last sermon. I could see Party authorities trying to break it up and keep the peace, but they could do nothing to quell the crowd.

A Christian from the Free German Youth said, "I'm a Christian, let me talk!" But they would have none of it. The Communists became louder and were grinding their teeth at us, their eyes wild with hatred. We had many young people, many girls, students, and new believers among us, and I felt responsible for each one. In seconds we could have been in a horrible riot.

I shouted to the Christians to start a human train, and I led the way. Each person held the one in front of him with both hands and we began to walk out through the massive crowd. I broke through the locked arms of the Communists and just kept walking, leading that huge train of believers from the center of the hostility.

As the Communists shoved and swung at me, I was overwhelmed with the joy of God. There had been many times in my ministry when I had been in less dangerous situations and had been terribly frightened. But this night, with what seemed like the whole Communist world throwing fists and elbows at me and bottling me in a mass of humanity, I got the holy giggles. I was joyous at being persecuted for Jesus. The words of the old lady's notebook from the night before came

147

back to me: "Blessed are you when men revile you . . ."

At the back of the huge crowd of Communists were delegates who still didn't know what was going on. All they knew was that the Free German Youth had the Jesus People cornered and trouble was brewing. They were not in a position to see us making our slow, winding escape through the crowd. It took about five minutes for the train of Christians to pull free from the middle. By that time, I, as the leader, had gone all the way to the edge of the crowd and was circling around the back. To people at the edge, I said, "Have you heard?"

They said, "No. What's going on?"

"Jesus loves you!" I said.

"Oh, no!" they wailed. "They're everywhere!"

Jesus had become the major issue on the last night of the Communist Youth World Fest. Mission: impossible. Mission: accomplished. We hardly slept that night, praising God and planning to stay a few more days to disciple the new believers.

Chapter Twenty-One

"DANKE, SOMMY"

During our last two days in Berlin, we spent several hours just fellowshipping with the believers and discipling them. Even during these times of worship, we saw two more kids, one a Marxist and the other an alcoholic, come and give their hearts to Jesus.

Fred and Fred had decided to stay in West Berlin to pack. Jeff and I went to spend eight hours praying and pouring the Word of God into the believers. Many of them rode the train back to the border with us. My heart broke as I thought about leaving them, and I wept. I understood how Paul must have felt when he left new bodies of believers he had helped originate. I wanted them to remain one in the Spirit so they would be able to stand in the evil day and hold fast to the testimony of Jesus Christ. Even as I think about that last day now, my heart just breaks.

We passed Alexanderplatz and I saw the sun reflecting our cross off the huge TV tower. "There is our church," I said.

"Yes," the young people said.

"And there is our steeple," I said.

"Yes," they answered. "And there are the people who need Jesus."

And I said, "Yes."

When we got back to the Temple of Tears where we would part, the last night of the festival filled my mind. My Czechoslovakia brother cried and said, "Sammy, do not forget us. When you come back, please come to Czechoslovakia. Our young people need to hear your preaching."

And there was Ilse. "Sommy," she said (all the German kids pronounced my name that way), "please come back. We need your leadership. We need the leadership of God in you."

Kids from the other countries, and from East Berlin gathered around and touched my shoulders and cried. "Sommy, please come back," they said. I cried and cried.

"Danke (thank you), Sommy," each said in turn, tears running down their faces. "Danke, Sommy."

"Danke, Jesus," I said to each, smiling through tears, my voice thick. "Danke, danke, Jesus." For it was He who had drawn them unto Himself. I knew they had met the resurrected Savior.

I left feeling like a father who must leave his spiritual children. I did not know what their futures held, but I knew their lives would each carry more difficulty and danger than mine. I praised God for their boldness.

Back in Frankfurt, we rejoiced with the brothers and sisters who had gone through agonizing intercessory prayer for us. I spent a few days there speaking and sharing the story of the Fest, and then it was back to America and the Gateway Baptist Church—back to the body of believers which had sent us out in the power and authority of God. All the way home, all I could think about were the brothers and sisters we had left behind. Our new friends in Christ. I knew that I would be returning to them soon. I just had to.

EPILOGUE

Sammy and his friends made two return trips behind the iron curtain, and despite hair-raising experiences and hassles (enough for another book!), he saw that the Holy Spirit is continuing a great work. Even in Czechoslovakia, from which he only narrowly escaped, the believers are being discipled and more are being won.

Sammy is planning yet another trip in 1975 to obey some leadings of God which are so heavy and so potentially explosive that I dare not even hint at them here. Besides Russia, he is looking also toward some of the Moslem countries which have been so tightly closed to the Gospel. The harvest is there and waiting to be picked.

Even if he is stopped from ministering the way he feels led, no one can stop the working of the Holy Spirit. Even now God may be speaking to your heart. Perhaps you will be one who will be chosen of Him to help carry on the ministry. If not behind the iron curtain, what about in your own community?

". . . The harvest truly is plenteous, but the labourers are few; pray ye therefore the Lord of the harvest, that he will send forth labourers into his harvest" (Matthew 9:37b, 38).

For further information regarding this ministry, please contact:

Sammy Tippit
Post Office Box 27175
San Antonio, Texas 78227

GOD'S LOVE IN ACTION, INC.
Sammy Tippit Ministries
1800 N.E. Loop 410   Suite 309
San Antonio, Texas 78217

Suggested Inspirational Paperback Books

FACE UP WITH A MIRACLE
by Don Basham
$1.25

This is a fascinating book about God the Holy Spirit bringing a new dimension into the lives of twentieth-century Christians. It is filled with experiences that testify to a God of miracles being unleashed in our lives right now.

BAPTISM IN THE HOLY SPIRIT: COMMAND OR OPTION? by Bob Campbell
$1.25

A teaching summary on the Holy Spirit, covering the three kinds of baptisms, the various workings of the Holy Spirit, the question of tongues and how to know when you have received the baptism of the Spirit.

A SCRIPTURAL OUTLINE OF THE BAPTISM IN THE HOLY SPIRIT
by George and Harriet Gillies
60¢

Here is a very brief and simple outline of the baptism in the Holy Spirit, with numerous references under each point. This handy little booklet is a good reference for any question you might have concerning this subject.

A HANDBOOK ON HOLY SPIRIT BAPTISM
by Don Basham
$1.25

Questions and answers on the baptism in the Holy Spirit and speaking in tongues. The book is in great demand, and answers many important questions from within the contemporary Christian Church.

HE SPOKE, AND I WAS STRENGTHENED
by Dick Mills
$1.25

An easy-to-read devotional of 52 prophetic scripturally-based messages directed to the businessman, the perfectionist, the bereaved, the lonely, the ambitious, and many more.

SEVEN TIMES AROUND
By Bob and Ruth McKee
$1.25

A Christan growth story of a family who receives the baptism in the Holy Spirit and then applies this new experience to solve the family's distressing, but frequently humorous, problems.

LET GO!
by Fenelon
95¢

Jesus promised a life full of joy and peace. Why then are so many Christians struggling to attain the qualities that Christ said belonged to the child of God? Fenelon speaks firmly—but lovingly—to those whose lives have been an uphill battle. Don't miss this one.

VISIONS BEYOND THE VEIL
by H. A. Baker
$1.25

Beggar children who heard the Gospel at a rescue mission in China received a powerful visitation of the Holy Spirit, during which they saw visions of heaven and Christ which cannot be explained away. A new revised edition.

DEAR DAD, THIS IS TO ANNOUNCE MY DEATH by Ric Kast
$1.25

The story of how rock music, drugs, and alcohol lead a youth to commit suicide. While Ric waits out the last moments of life, Jesus Christ rescues him from death and gives him a new life.

GATEWAY TO POWER
by Wesley Smith
$1.25

From the boredom of day after day routine and lonely nights of meaningless activity, Wes Smith was caught up into a life of miracles. Dramatic healings, remarkable financial assistance, and exciting escapes from dangerous situations have become part of his life.

SIGI AND I
by Gwen Schmidt
95¢

The intriguing narrative of how two women smuggled Bibles and supplies to Christians behind the Iron Curtain. An impressive account of their simple faith in following the Holy Spirit.

SPIRITUAL POWER
by Don Basham

$1.25

Over 100 received new spiritual power after hearing the author give this important message. The book deals with such topics as the baptism as a second experience, the primary evidence of the baptism, and tongues and the "Chronic Seeker."

THE LAST CHAPTER
by A. W. Rasmussen

$1.45

An absorbing narrative based on the author's own experience in the charismatic renewal around the world. He presents many fresh insights on fasting, Church discipline, and Christ's Second Coming.

A HANDBOOK ON TONGUES, INTERPETATION AND PROPHECY by Don Basham

$1.25

The second of Don Basham's Handbook series. Again set up in the convenient question and answer format, the book addresses itself to further questions on the Holy Spirit, especially the vocal gifts.